POSTCARDS FROM ABROAD

Postcards from Abroad opens with a description of an early contested election for International President of the writer's organisation, PEN, during which one of the delegates, disagreeing with the voting procedure, made off with the ballot papers and was angrily pursued down the hall by the International Secretary. The author was in a good position to observe this and other bizarre happenings in the life of PEN during the twenty-nine years she spent working at the organisation's London headquarters. In this perceptive memoir she relives twenty of those years (1968 to 1988), when the organisation was in the process of developing from its intimate beginnings in the 'Twenties to the worldwide status it holds today. Whilst not ignoring PEN's noble ideals of the defence of freedom of expression and friendship between writers regardless of frontiers and political alignments, she chooses to concentrate on the lighter side of the life of the organisation, describing with gentle irony the often eccentric characters she has met and worked with, and the adventures, sometimes hilarious, which take place at the annual gatherings of writers from all over the world at the PEN Congresses.

After a country childhood in Sussex Elizabeth Paterson took a degree in English at St. Andrews University in Scotland and did a variety of jobs, both in England and abroad before, in 1968, she found her true vocation at the London headquarters of the writers' organisation, International PEN. For twenty-nine years she was involved in all the aspects of the work of that remarkable organisation, relishing both its achievements and its eccentricities. When she retired in 1997 she spent a pleasurable time reliving some of those exhilarating, exasperating and fascinating years in writing this book. She now divides her time between London and the New Forest.

"*Postcards from Abroad* has given me pleasure, fun and revelations about some PEN members and, most charmingly, of the author. What a joy to discover a WRITER." **Sybille Bedford**

"Elizabeth Paterson's memoir is an important literary document in its own right, as well as being slyly – and sometimes openly – amusing . . ." **Antonia Fraser**

"This is a beautifully written memoir of an important and often eccentric organisation. Elizabeth Paterson is a wonderfully astute observer and her book is revealing, funny and, above all, immensely readable." **Ronald Harwood**

"This book reminded me of so much I had almost forgotten, but in a witty and descriptive manner that I greatly enjoyed . . ." **Arthur Miller**

"A book to relish, told with humour, affection and friendly gossip." **Bernice Rubens**

G000144026

ELIZABETH PATERSON

Postcards from Abroad

MEMORIES OF PEN

Poets, Playwrights, Editors, Essayists
and Novelists

'Nothing from China. Nothing from Peru.
I'm therefore hoping that you are at home
And happily at work . . . I must have had postcards
From you over the years from nearly every country
In the world, but I'm sure you'll find many
other spots yet.'

Letter to the author from Kevin FitzGerald, November 1988

SINCLAIR STEVENSON

First published in Great Britain by
Sinclair-Stevenson
3 South Terrace, London SW7 2TB

Copyright © 2001 by Elizabeth Paterson

Extracts from Postcards from Abroad
have previously appeared in PEN *International magazine* and in
Confrontation, the literary magazine of Long Island University.

British Library Cataloguing in Publication Data.
A CIP catalogue record for this book is available from
The British Library.

ISBN 0 953 73987 2

Typeset by Rowland Phototypesetting Ltd., Bury St Edmunds, Suffolk.
Printed and bound by St Edmundsbury Press, Bury St Edmunds, Suffolk.

FOR PETER ELSTOB
who shared most of these adventures and
encouraged me to write about them

PROLOGUE

To start in the middle: it was September 1971, a golden autumn in Ireland, and International PEN was holding its Dublin Congress. A hundred or more writers from all over the world were assembled in the conference room of the Royal Marine Hotel, Dun Laoghaire, in the process of electing a new International President. In the chair was the irascible Belgian lawyer and poet, Robert Goffin; beside him, the International Secretary, David Carver, an imposing figure, counting the votes. I too was up on the platform in my usual position, sitting at David's right hand, taking the Minutes. I had just jotted down the number of votes for each candidate as David announced them: 20 for the incumbent president, the temperamental French poet Pierre Emmanuel; 25 for the self-effacing German novelist Heinrich Böll (not yet a Nobel Prize winner). There were cheers from Heinrich's many supporters, but discontent on the francophone side, when suddenly Christophe Assamoi, the portly Secretary of the Côte d'Ivoire PEN Centre, saying that David's counting of the votes should be checked, nipped up to the front of the hall, seized the voting slips from the dais and made off with them with surprising agility and speed. He was hotly pursued by David, also no light weight, who pounded down the hall after him, purple in the face with rage, shouting: "Come back Monsieur Assamoi. Come back at once!".

I will describe the end of this farcical incident in its due place, but first a little more about PEN and how I came to find myself on that platform in Dun Laoghaire.

"Personal Secretary required for General Secretary of International Writers' organisation. Opportunities for travel and meeting writers. Applications to PEN, 62 Glebe Place, Chelsea, SW3."

It was in the summer of 1968 that this advertisement in the personal column of *The Times* caught my eye. It interested me because at the age of 34 I still had not settled on a permanent career. I had a good degree in English from St. Andrew's University and twelve years' experience in a variety of secretarial jobs, both in England and Canada, so I felt I should be equipped to do this one and it might be just what I was looking for. But what was PEN?

From a reference library I discovered that it should more correctly be written P.E.N., an acronym for Poets, Playwrights, Editors,

Essayists and Novelists, that it had been founded in 1921 by an English novelist called Amy Dawson Scott, and that there were P.E.N. Centres all over the world. Equipped with this scanty information, I went to Chelsea for interview.

After I had got the job I gradually discovered that Mrs. Dawson Scott's brainchild, born of the spirit of internationalism which succeeded the horrors of the First World War and founded as a sort of dining club for foreign writers visiting London, had developed into a mini-United Nations, but representing literatures and languages rather than nations. It had also become a defender of free expression, most notably at a Congress in Dubrovnik in 1933, held under the chairmanship of the then International President, H. G. Wells, when the German delegation had been called to account (and subsequently expelled) for not protesting against Hitler's Burning of the Books. It had taken on its role as a defender also of imprisoned writers and journalists four years later when it had successfully appealed to General Franco for the release of Arthur Koestler who, in Spain on behalf of the *News Chronicle*, had been arrested in Malaga and condemned to death. Because it was apolitical it managed, in the Cold War days when I first became acquainted with it, to retain Centres behind the Iron Curtain as well as a Centre for Writers in Exile which largely consisted of refugees from those countries. In 1980 it was the first international organisation to have Centres in Mainland China and in Taiwan; in 1992 it was the first to have a Centre for Palestinian Writers as well as an Israeli Centre.

Of course it has not always managed to live up to all the admirable tenets of its Charter,* but it has done remarkably well both in greatly developing its role as a defender of freedom of expression through its Writers in Prison Committee and in acting as a meeting ground for writers and intellectuals across political divides. It is not sufficiently well-known in Britain, but in Eastern Europe and Asia, for instance, it is a name to conjure with.

For me it became for twenty-nine exhausting, maddening, hilarious and exciting years a way of life, indeed an addiction, which has brought me great pleasure and wonderful friendships. Now I am retired I have been self-indulgently reliving some of those years by writing down my memories of them. Some serious histories of PEN have already been written, and more remain to be written. This is a light-hearted and very personal memoir of a unique and remarkable organisation.

---

* See Appendix

Part I

DAVID CARVER
"A Great Personal Success"

1

"You know of course that we're the only international writers' organisation?", David Carver said, scrutinising me from the other side of his director's desk.

The sun was shining in at the long windows of his office on the first floor of Glebe House. "This building is rather small to house the offices of the English Centre and be the headquarters of the whole organisation," he went on, "but we intend to take on the lease of the derelict studio next door and turn the whole premises into a writers' house."

Formerly a professional lieder singer, David was General Secretary of International PEN and of the English Centre of PEN, both of which posts had been bequeathed to him by his friend Hermon Ould. He was large, florid, well-groomed and wore Savile Row suits cut to minimise his bulk. His occasional pomposity was counterbalanced by a witty turn of phrase and he could be very amusing company when he was in the mood. He was an impressive performer at meetings of the International Executive Committee, where he had only to look over his half-glasses at a recalcitrant delegate to bring him or her to heel. As a last resort he would go purple in the face and threaten to resign, and that stratagem never failed to get him his way. In English PEN he tended to be surrounded by a clique – largely female – and not to waste much time on those outside it, but internationally he was very popular and greatly respected. Over the six years I worked for him I passed from admiration to disillusionment, to irritated affection and sympathy.

When interviewing me he showed surprisingly little interest in my qualifications and, since I reckon that I never appear at my best at interviews, I was puzzled to know what decided him to select me over the other applicants for the job. It was only later that Gwyneth Cooper, widow of the playwright Giles Cooper, told me that David had telephoned her as one of my referees and they had had a long talk. Since I was working for Giles in 1966 when he was killed by falling from a train and I had spent some harrowing weeks helping Gwyneth in the aftermath of the tragedy, I suppose she was able to testify to my stamina in a crisis – of which I was to encounter many in my time with PEN!

Glebe House, PEN's headquarters at the time when I joined the staff, was a handsome building in Chelsea. It was really two houses (numbers 62 and 63) awkwardly joined into one, parts of number 63 dating back to the late seventeenth century. It was the property of the Church Commissioners and had been leased to Henrietta Leslie, a faithful member of English PEN. She, on her death, had left the remainder of the lease to PEN Above the office on the first floor where David presided there was a self-contained flat, then let to two hairdressers, Emile Riley and his beautiful blonde boyfriend. On the ground floor there was a large, gloomy reception room, always called the Board Room, and, opening off the back of the Board room, the "Vine Room", which had once been a Huguenot chapel and had a fig tree growing up through the floor and spreading its branches under the glass-domed roof. It was a very charming room, a great feature of PEN parties and only spoiled by a pervading smell of cats which apparently emanated from the fig. The front door of 62 Glebe Place gave on to a small hall which connected with the Board Room and from which a steep staircase went up to the two small and shabby offices which housed the staff.

This was in keeping with David's large ideas of what was due to PEN and to himself. There was his Personal Assistant, Liz Warner, a friend of Rosamond Lehmann's, who had been an actress and a talented pianist and was also an excellent cook. She had for a time been Rex Warner's common law wife and had changed her name to his. Her chief function in PEN was as David's social secretary and adviser, although she had been officially engaged (by courtesy of a grant obtained for the purpose) to sort out the archives for possible sale to the University of Texas, via the booksellers Bertram Rota. She later ran the Glebe House restaurant and bar, during its brief and financially disastrous life. One of her regular tasks was to telephone Alexandre Blokh (then Head of the Cultural Division at Unesco) and his wife Nadia at their house in the Rue des Orchidées to forewarn them of David's impending arrival in Paris for a Unesco meeting. This was intended to ensure that they would invite him to dinner. She used to groan over this task, which she found embarrassing, but as far as I know the dinner invitation was always forthcoming, and the aura of glamour which somehow surrounded these events was my first association with the Blokhs.

Lizzie Bradish-Ellames, an attractive blonde, who was also connected with Rosamond Lehmann through her father (a retired cavalry officer generally known as "The Major") who had once been briefly married to Rosamond's sister Helen, was Secretarial Assistant. There was also a long-legged and beautiful girl called Teresa Bantock (known by her family nickname of "Trees") who worked the switchboard and did David's shopping at Harrod's. There was also a shifting population of book-keepers, since the entanglement of International and English PEN's accounts was so daunting that confrontation with it tended to lead to nervous breakdown and speedy departure. Also on the strength was Kate Nott, the distinguished philosopher, novelist and poet, who edited the PEN magazine, which in those days was called *The Bulletin of Selected Books*, and frequented Glebe House meetings and parties as well as regularly attending all international meetings. Last there was Beatrice Darbon (always known as "Dorrit" because of her diminutive size) who had been housekeeper to Henrietta Leslie and bequeathed by her to PEN. Dorrit and her very shy husband, Nelson, inhabited the two rooms at the back of No. 62, which opened onto the courtyard where the mulberry trees planted by the Huguenots grew. Apart from doing all the cleaning, dusting and polishing, she also washed David's silver-backed hairbrushes, served his Earl Grey tea, had a biscuit tin which was generously at the disposal of hungry office staff, and always produced delicious, but very crumbly mincepies for the staff Christmas party. She was also a good source of information on earlier PEN scandals, such as when a former Personal Assistant of David's (male) had seduced one of the girls in the office, having assignations with her in the Vine Room. David had been afraid that the girl's father, a retired colonel, would hold him personally responsible and would come up from the country with a horse whip!

2

There were regular meetings of the English Centre members in the Board Room, parties in the Vine Room, and monthly meetings of its Executive Committee, nominally presided over by L. P. Hartley, but actually under the firm control of David Carver, who would turn to his President occasionally and say: "I'm sure you agree with me, Leslie". It was my job to take the Minutes, so I sat at a table beside the President and Secretary. L. P. Hartley, who looked like an amiable sea-lion, always greeted me on his arrival with the utmost courtesy and as if he had never seen me before in his life. Lizzie Bradish-Ellames told me how, on one occasion when he was just climbing into his car to leave Glebe House, his manservant in Bath had telephoned. Lizzie had offered to run out and give Mr. Hartley a message and the manservant had said: "Just ask him whether the answer's yes or no." On receipt of this message Leslie Hartley, looking totally bemused, had said: "Yes or no? Yes or no? ... Oh well, say yes." The manservant's delight led Lizzie to suppose that he had either been given a rise or some time off. Leslie was always being cheated by his menservants (he had one in London and one in Bath) and usually ended up visiting them in prison ("poking cigarettes through the bars", according to David).

My happiest memory of him is when, as President of English PEN, he took the chair at a dinner for the visiting delegates of other Centres who had come to London for a meeting of the International Executive Committee (probably the one in March 1969). In David's day such events were conducted in the grand style, regardless of expense, so it took place at the Criterion, with a toastmaster in charge of proceedings. Leslie Hartley appeared to be enjoying his dinner except when galvanised by the toastmaster to get up and say something. First he had to make a speech welcoming the guests, but his pronunciation of their names was so eccentric that most of them didn't realise that they had been welcomed. Then he had to reply to a long and eloquent speech by the President of French PEN, Yves Gandon. To the great amusement of the French Ambassador, who was seated on his right as the guest of honour, he said, after a long pause for thought: ". . . I don't actually understand spoken French, but I know from reading it that it is a very logical language, so I'm sure that Monsieur Gandon has made a very logical speech . . ." Yves Gandon, whose knowledge of English was even less than Leslie Hartley's of French, smiled happily, convinced that he was being suitably thanked.

*

The members of the English PEN Committee were expected to sit meekly in rows in the Board Room under David's commanding eye and keep quiet unless asked to speak. The chief rebel was Peter Elstob (military historian, novelist, entrepreneur – of whom much more later), always the naughty boy in the class, who was not deterred from asking awkward questions by the disapproval of David's adoring female coterie. He was backed up by Nicolette Devas.

Nicolette had had an unconventional childhood in the Augustus John household (vividly described in her book *Two Flamboyant Fathers*) and, like Peter, had an enquiring and irreverent mind. She was also a very friendly person and I soon found myself invited round to delicious suppers in the basement kitchen of the tall house in Limerston Street where she lived with her artist husband Rupert Shephard. Rupert was in fact the second artist she had married; her first had been the portrait painter Anthony Devas. She and Rupert had known each other when they were students at The Slade, and had married late in life when they had each lost their first partners. There were grown up children from both families who seemed to mingle happily at the large and lively parties which Nicolette gave. I first got to know Rupert as a tall and rubicund figure, with a shock of white hair standing gloomily on the outskirts of Glebe House parties. I found him very difficult to talk to until I discovered that the secret was to ply him with a stiff gin, when he immediately livened up. Their domestic calm had occasionally been punctuated, in the early days of their marriage, by the eruption onto the scene of Nicolette's sister Caitlin and her husband Dylan Thomas arriving drunk in the small hours and throwing pebbles at their window to rouse them.

It was because of Nicolette's connection with PEN that Glebe House was chosen as the venue for the reception when Dylan and Caitlin's daughter, Aeronwy Thomas, got married. Liz Warner took on the catering and, since the bridegroom was an enthusiastic rugger player, produced a cake which represented a rugger field, complete with goal posts and two opposing teams. According to Liz's account, the reception must have been a strange occasion. The Saturday afternoon peace of Glebe Place was shattered by the roistering of the bridegroom's rugger-playing friends whilst, by contrast, his mother and her friends, who were deaf mutes, were happily conversing in sign language.

The other unbeliever on the English PEN Committee was that delightful Irishman Kevin FitzGerald (writer, rock climber and raconteur), who, folding his long limbs (he was over six foot) into the back row, watched the proceedings with a friendly but sardonic eye and as soon as I got to know him – which was very soon – started writing me ironic and very funny descriptions of David's method of handling the Committee. This was the beginning of a correspondence which endured, in spite of his increasing ill health and eventual blindness, until his death at the age of ninety-one in 1993, and was a continuing delight to me. His view of the Committee was shown in the letter he wrote to Peter when Peter stepped into David's shoes in 1974: "I hope you are enjoying PEN and being the Sovereign Pontiff. I long to hear your version of David's, 'That's a particularly foolish question, Felicity'."

Chief among the faithful was Mary Treadgold, one of the more wealthy and elegant members of PEN and one of its benefactors. She had been a producer and literary editor at the BBC and had written some novels and several children's books, but to me she was known for her first book, *We Mustn't Leave Dinah*. This dramatic account of the rescue of a pony from the Channel Islands before the German invasion had appeared in 1941 and had been given to me for my eighth birthday. I had loved it, but when I met Mary I found it difficult to imagine her being able to relate to children like the pony-mad young girl who was the heroine of that book. But then, as Josephine Pullein-Thompson, also an author of pony books but a very different personality, later explained to me, Mary must have been drawing on her own childhood rather then empathising with present-day children.

A more sympathetic character – also a children's writer – was Dorothy Clewes, a jolly, sturdily-built lady who had an ex officio position as Chair of the House Committee (a post whose duties Kevin described as "doing the flowers") and loyally came up from the heart of Sussex for every meeting. My chief memory of her is bound up with the start of my disillusionment with David. It was at the Annual General Meeting, which was always held at The English-Speaking Union in December. Or at least it was held there every year except the one in question, which I think was possibly 1969, when it had to be postponed at the last moment because David had not got round to writing his Secretary's Report. His decision to postpone the meeting was taken too late to inform the membership, so he decreed that he and I would together go down to the English-Speaking Union to lie in wait for and placate any members who turned up. I went with him reluctantly and was dumbfounded and furious when, upon Dorothy Clewes' arrival, David immediately, without any apology to me, hailed her off for a drink, leaving me alone in the firing line. Fortunately not many members ever came to the A.G.M. in those days and those who did were mostly Londoners, but one country member did arrive and was naturally enraged to be told that his long journey had been in vain. He reluctantly accepted my excuses, but declared angrily that if David had been there he would have punched him on the nose. I felt that David had displayed discretion rather than valour!

*

The Thomas wedding reception was an unusual event. In general, apart from the Christmas Party, the big annual do at Glebe House was the launch of the *New Poems* anthology which English PEN used to publish in conjunction with Hutchinsons. Although David had a very low opinion of poets as a race, he would not have considered it proper to have given them only wine with Dorrit's canapes, so there was a plentiful supply of hard liquor, still remembered nostalgically by the poets of that generation. When they were finally turned out into Glebe Place, they most of them staggered off to finish the evening in the nearest pub.

Dinners took place at the Cock Tavern in Fleet Street, where the food was very bad, but the atmosphere suitably literary. The tables were arranged in an E shape, with the speaker seated in the middle of the long side of the E, with his back to the wall. My clearest memory of these not usually very dynamic occasions was of an evening when P. H. Newby was speaking, chaired by Gerda Charles, and I was sitting next to Irene Rathbone. Irene was a delightful but eccentric elderly member, a novelist and poet, who had been a friend of Nancy Cunard, a passionate francophone and great admirer of Louis Aragon. She had trained for the stage when she was young and so the supposedly *sotto voce* comments which she was inclined to make on public occcasions were sometimes disastrously audible. She had been lectured by Liz Warner on this propensity and told to write her comments down instead of speaking them. Unfortunately on this occasion she had been placed on the speaker's left hand and, since he was standing up to deliver his talk, he probably had quite a clear aerial view of her scribblings on her programme card. Certainly I thought his voice faltered when she wrote against his name: "Small, brown and *un*distinguished".

3

That Glebe House was not merely a pleasant social centre for English writers, but the hub of an international organisation which has since its foundation been a microcosm of world events was forcefully demonstrated very shortly after I started work there. In that same month, August 1968, the Russians invaded Czechoslovakia and David, deciding that this represented an extreme form of censorship of Czech and Slovak writers, requested every PEN Centre to send a telegram of support to their beleaguered colleagues in Prague. This, in the days before faxes, involved Teresa sitting at the switchboard for hours on end, supplied with endless cups of coffee and wearing out shifts of telegraph operators, as she dictated the addresses of all the Centres, sending each one the same message.

The Russian invasion of Czechoslovakia and PEN's reaction to it was the most hotly canvassed question at my first International PEN meeting, a Conference which took place in Geneva from October 6th to 8th of that year. Arthur Miller, in his last year as International President, chaired the International Executive Committee, at which Jiri Mucha and Marta Kadlecikova (whom I chiefly remember for her stylish boots) were the centre of attention, since they had come from the Czechoslovak Centre. They were present only as observers rather than delegates, because of the dangers of their position when they returned home, and were usually in the company of their countryman Pavel Tigrid, who lived in Paris and was in those days a regular delegate for the Writers in Exile Centre (after the Velvet Revolution he returned to Prague as Vaclav Havel's first Minister of Culture).

Apart from the dramas in the Executive Committee my chief recollections of the Geneva Conference are of its extreme disorganisation. The unseasonable heat of the autumn sun beat on the picture windows of the small office in the Hôtel du Rhône, where Liz Warner, Lizzie Bradish-Ellames and I tried to unscramble the hopeless muddle of the hotel bookings. Jean-Theodore Brutsch, the Secretary of the Centre Suisse Romande, had assured David that all the arrangements had been made, but we quickly found that, because the poor man had suffered a slight stroke and refused to allow anyone else from his Centre to help him, the arrangements had been made in his head rather than in fact. Mary Treadgold had come along to the Conference in attendance on David and I have an unlikely vision of her loitering in the lobby of the Hotel de Rhone wearing her mink coat (surely this must be a trick of my imagination seeing how hot the weather was) whilst we struggled with the hotel bookings. I do remember that she wanted Liz to come for an outing on the lake with her, an invitation which Liz virtuously refused.

Some frivolous memories of that strange week: Henry Williamson and Petronella O'Flanagan (an Irish woman broadcaster with an eccentric line in hats and a remarkable head for whisky) duelling with table knives over lunch and Henry throwing bread rolls in the air and catching them in his mouth, to the astonished disapproval of the respectable burghers of Geneva who surrounded us. Having a dinner of "hot ham" with Per Wästberg (the new President of Swedish PEN), his then wife, Anna-Lena, and the American delegate, Robert Halsband, on our way to a marvellous candlelit concert in the Museum of Ancient Instruments. Introducing myself rather naively to André Chamson as "the new secretary", to which he courteously responded: "And I am the old President", Peter Elstob delighting the elderly ladies of English PEN, on departure, by lining them up in military fashion beside their luggage to make sure all were present and correct.

The Scottish PEN, represented in Geneva by two notable Glaswegians, was always in those days very much a focal point of the social life of any international meeting. Cliff Hanley, whose dimunitive size bore no relation to the multiplicity of his talents: novelist, journalist, author of *Scotland the Brave* and of a delightful account of his childhood in the Gorbals called *Dancing in the Streets*, was regarded with deep suspicion by David as a Left Wing rebel – a Red very much not under the bed. And, speaking of beds, Cliff found that the one compensation of the rather sleazy hotel which had been allocated to him was that his bed was equipped with a vibrator. He obeyed the instructions and put ten francs in the slot, but, greatly to his annoyance, nothing happened, until the middle of the night, when he was woken unceremoniously by what he thought at first must be an earthquake.

The other Scottish delegate was Lavinia Derwent, author of *Tammy Troot* and other children's books, and well-known Scottish TV personality, whose exuberance I at first found rather overwhelming. It was only later that I came to realise that, behind this front, she was really a very private person, but someone whose warmth and kindness enabled her to surmount or disregard barriers of race and language. It was Lavinia who invented the PEN bedroom party, at which a random selection of delegates were invited to bring their toothmugs to one of the Scottish delegates' hotel rooms and pool their duty-free Scotch. Many friendships were formed in this way and many possible disagreements in the Executive Committee averted. International PEN meetings have not been the same since 1983, the year when Lavinia had the stroke that prevented her from coming again and led eventually to her death.

According to the invariable custom of International PEN meetings in those days, the fine weather lasted whilst we were cooped up in the Hotel du Rhone having meetings, but broke spectacularly on the final day, when we were taken on an excursion on the lake to see Madame de Stael's chateau. I remember a very ladylike member of English PEN, Katharine Morris, being overcome with embarrassment and profuse apologies when, putting up her umbrella rather too hastily for the dash from the chateau to the boat, she somehow managed to get it entangled in the elaborate coiffure of an elderly and tiresome member of the host Centre, who positively hissed with rage in response. David, Rosamond Lehmann and Kate Nott had meanwhile stayed on board the boat drinking whisky and greeted our bedraggled return with aggravating superiority.

*

to KEVIN FITZGERALD   *Menton*
Crossways, Chinnor, Oxon   *September 1969*

Dear Kevin,
At that very entertaining lunch you treated me to at the Athenaeum (Ladies' Annexe) last month I promised to send you a p.p.c from our next Congress. So, here we are in Menton, with the sun shining on us. I've been quartered in a small hotel some way from the Conference Centre with a nice Estonian couple from London and a Japanese lady who bows and smiles charmingly, but evidently doesn't understand a word of English. Every time I tell her that the bus is here to take us to the Conference Centre she leaps into the lift and disappears to her room. The Helbemaes and I spend a lot of time trying to shepherd her in the right direction. Much love, Elizabeth

At the Menton Congress Arthur Miller relinquished the International Presidency to Pierre Emmanuel. Arthur was an excellent chairman, brisk but fair, but didn't set much store by the ceremonial side of his office. I remember that when we were all lined up outside the Conference Centre in Menton to welcome the Mayor, some official suddenly noticed that Arthur wasn't wearing a tie, and one had to be snatched from a bystander and pressed upon him. I also remember that he took Lizzie out to dinner up in the hills behind the town when he was supposed to be fulfilling some official engagement.

True to precedent, the sun shone idyllically on the Côte d'Azur whilst we were confined to the Conference Centre, and even for our half-day's visit to Monte Carlo, but when we embarked from Nice to sail to Corsica on the post-Congress outing the skies were grey, and as we came down the gangplank at Ajaccio the heavens opened and we were drenched. By the time we got to Napoleon's birthplace dusk was setting in and, there being no electric lighting installed there, we got a rather dim view of it. We were then all piled into a coach and driven off, still sodden, into the darkness for at least an hour to what we discovered in the next morning's sunlight to be a sort of holiday camp, beautifully situated on a sandy beach. By that stage we weren't bothered about the surroundings, only about having a wash, finding a bed and eating some dinner, but all these goals proved difficult to achieve. The bedroom huts were not designed for single guests, but for families – one double bed and three bunks in each – and in any case they had all been pre-booked by some other organisation before French PEN booked them for us. So, as a dejected procession of PEN delegates collected keys from the reception desk and sloshed off down the paved paths to the bedroom huts which they thought had been allocated to them, only to find them already allocated to someone else, to return for another key and repeat the experience. Lizzie and I gave up all hope of sleeping anywhere except on the floor. However, as I was leaning against the reception desk observing the chaos, David came up to me and asked me in a stage whisper whether I had anywhere to sleep. When I said no, he revealed that he had a whole bedroom hut to himself and so, with rare generosity, he offered to take Lizzie and me in with him (we sleeping chastely in the bunks, whilst he occupied the double bed) provided that we told no-one. I think I kept my word, but it was certainly the talk of the Congress next day that David had slept not only with one, but with both, of his secretaries.

Everyone found somewhere to sleep in the end, although there were some very odd pairings off, and wild tales went the rounds about delegates who had offered money to others to give up their beds, and of one delegate who had vanished into the night and was never seen again. Finally, about 9 o'clock we all sat down to a very good dinner of wild boar, over which Pierre Emmanuel made his acceptance speech. From subsequent experience I suspect it was not just the fact that we were all absolutely exhausted that made his speech seem so unconscionably long. Somehow we survived it and staggered off to bed.

When we woke the next morning the sun was sparkling on the sea and the previous night's adventures seemed like a bad dream. After breakfast we got back into our coach and were driven over the mountains and up to Bastia at the northern end of the island, where we embarked again for Nice and the plane for home.

4

In 1970 there were various staff changes at Glebe House. Lizzie "heard the call of the wild" (in David's phrase) and left to get a job in Australia (later returning to marry John Harvey, of Harvey's Bristol Cream). She was replaced by Katie Ryde, daughter of Peter Ryde, *The Times'* golf correspondent, and granddaughter of *The Telegraph's* veteran theatre critic, W. A. Darlington. The Darlington family had been very friendly with the Milnes, and Katie's mother, Anne, was the little girl in the buttercup meadow with Christopher Robin in "Now We Are Six". Sadly, she had died when Katie and her sister were quite small, so they had been brought up by their father, living round the corner from PEN in Phene Street. Katie when she started work at PEN was a complete contrast to Lizzie, shy and serious. Lizzie had been well-endowed with savoir faire; Katie had a much more intellectual bent. She had ambitions to be a writer, so she was quickly at home in PEN She was also very able and efficient and I was very sorry when she eventually left in 1975 to find more scope for her talents.

Teresa overlapped with Katie for a few months and then announced that one of her boyfriends had offered her a better-paid job selling Morgan sports cars. She arranged for her landlady, who wanted a part-time job, to come for interview. I had gathered from Teresa that Gertrude Thomson was an unusual person, and David, one of whose virtues was a very shrewd assessment of character, must have realised at once that he was in the presence of a remarkable woman. He engaged her on the spot and said: "I shall call you Gertie", so Gertie she became. She was a handsome woman of great presence who must then have been over sixty, because her previous job (as secretary to the Matron of an NHS hospital) had necessitated her lying about her age and dying her hair, which she wore in a bun on top of her head like a good German hausfrau. She was in fact half German and half English, her father having been an Englishman who went out to Silesia to manage the estate of a landowner there and married a local girl. Gertie was brought up in Silesia (then Germany, now Poland) until the age of eighteen, when she was sent to London to stay with her English relations. She spent the rest of her life in England, but never lost her German accent. Having had a disastrous first marriage to an impecunious antique dealer and having lost a baby, she met and married A. R. Thomson, the deaf and dumb portrait painter, by whom she had two children, Mary and Charles. When she met "Tommy" he was a successful commercial artist, but, having been told by his friends that he was capable of better things, she put her mind to altering his status to that of a portrait painter. Since she was a woman of determination who usually achieved what she set out to do, Tommy ended up a Royal Academician who was commissioned to do such prestigious jobs as group portraits of the House of Lords and the House of Commons, and the 40th Anniversary Dinner of the R.A.F., all of which necessitated a procession of V.I.P.'s coming to the shabby studio in Fernshaw Road, including most of the Royal Family. Gertie was no respecter of persons and had a beady eye for any signs of vanity or pomposity in her distinguished visitors (such as disagreements with the Clerk of the House's allocation of Front Bench seats in the portrait of the House of Lords). Of the Queen, however, she had nothing but good to say. The day Her Majesty was to come to the studio the Thomsons had been warned that strict secrecy must be preserved, but the presence of two large security men trying to conceal themselves behind inadequate bushes alerted the neighbours to some unusual happening long before the Queen arrived. She came in a plain car, carrying her tiara in a cardboard box. "I find it attracts less attention", she said.

In spite of her straitlaced appearance, Gertie was very worldly-wise and an extremely entertaining colleague, who became a great friend of mine. She swiftly realised that David's cherished Project for a Writers' House was never going to come to anything. She had no qualms, therefore, in suggesting to her son Charles, a repairer of antique clocks, that he should take over the top maisonette in 63 Glebe Place when the hairdresser Emile Riley, moved out, paying a small rent in consideration of putting the place back into good repair, and agreeing to move out as soon as The Project came to fruition. So Charles moved in, with a succession of attractive girl friends and a collection of pets (a rescued stray dog called Fred, one or two cats, and some gerbils). After he had been there some time and had done all the repairs, he was asked by David to move out so that, in accordance with a plan hatched by David and Liz Warner, the maisonette could be converted for Sybille Bedford, who had spent a great deal of money on architect's plans on their assurance that there would be no problem about her gaining possession. Charles, however, refused to move out and was accused by David of breaching a gentlemen's agreement. The resulting dispute led to bad blood, and, to my dismay, Gertie left in a rage. Luckily she didn't include me in her anger, and I used often to drop in at the Studio at 2 Fernshaw Road for supper and the latest gossip.

She not only helped me choose my first house (5 Rosebury Road in Fulham), but also helped me furnish it, taking me round second-hand furniture shops and fiercely forbidding me to open my mouth whilst she beat down the prices the dealers were asking. Among her many talents, she was an excellent cook and used to enjoy catering for my Writers' Day parties given at Rosebury Road (and afterwards at 14 Knivet Road) for the visitors from abroad.

But, to go back to 1970. The other great change in life at Glebe House was the retirement to Brighton of Dorrit and Nelson in the autumn of that year. David and Liz Warner evolved another plan, this time to turn the Darbons' quarters into a small bar and restaurant for PEN members. However, whilst they were waiting for this scheme to materialise there was an empty room in No. 62 and no-one to do the cleaning. Then one day Liz, looking over the back wall, found herself nose to nose with her cousin, Ian Campbell, who, unbeknownst to her, was living in a house on Oakley Street whose garden backed onto the Glebe House courtyard. Ian was a charming, feckless gay who had pretensions to be an artist. Since he was always short of money he was delighted to accept free accommodation in Glebe House in exchange for some housework. He enjoyed polishing the antique furniture, but was not always so keen on taking up David's afternoon tea, since four o'clock tended to be the best time for painting the sunset from the Albert Bridge – most of his paintings were of sunsets – but nevertheless he was amusing to have about the place. Gertie even forgave him when he asked her, quite without malice, which side she had been on in the war. He and Katie on one occasion got together to give a dinner in the vine room for the staff. I remember that the dessert was a very good meringue concoction made with mulberries from the trees in the yard.

5

The Seoul Congress was organised by the great lady of Korean PEN,
Miss Youn-Sook Moh, and David travelled to it in state, accompanied
by an entourage consisting of Liz Warner, Kate Nott, Peter Elstob (as
Press Officer) and me, joined en route by Leo Labedz, the Polish expert
on foreign affairs and Editor of the magazine *Survey*, whom David
treated as his own personal think tank.

Since this was my first visit to the Far East and was to include stops
in Hong Kong and Tokyo, as well as attendance at the Third Asian
Writers' Conference in Taipei en route for Seoul, and visits to The
Philippines and Ceylon on the way home, I obviously realised that it
was going to be a unique experience and, for once in my life at PEN
I kept a diary. Headed *Diary of Asian Tour 1970*, it starts by record-
ing, on June 15, our departure from Heathrow, which in my case
nearly did not happen:

> "I was just on my way to the Ladies when I bumped into David,
> who told me firmly that I must ring up the office and tell them
> that Noel Streatfeild had agreed to be hostess at the Midsummer
> Cocktail Party. What he didn't tell me was that our flight had
> just been called, so there was I queueing up to transmit this vital
> message and would have missed the plane if Kate and Liz had
> not spotted me and got me through the gate just in time. The
> men, needless to say, had gone ahead regardless."

I go on to record our flight to Hong Kong "cooped up like battery hens and being fed at far too frequent intervals as we kept overtaking the sun". We made slow progress, touching down at Frankfurt, Rome, Karachi and Bangkok and stopping for about twenty minutes at each.

"TUESDAY, 16 JUNE
We touched down at Karachi some time in the early hours of the morning and had our first taste of the tropics. Getting out of the plane was like emerging into a nightmare of shattering aircraft noise and damp heat that pressed down upon one so that it almost stopped one breathing . . . We reached Bangkok by the middle of the morning – in blazing heat. Nothing to be seen of the city, but very fine jewelry and souvenirs on sale in the airport building and a model of the ceremonial barge.

After Bangkok we flew over Cambodia and Vietnam, but all I saw of Vietnam was beautiful deserted beaches of white sand. Then we flew out over the South China Sea until we sighted the scattered islands of Hong Kong and dropped rapidly down to the airport. It was four o'clock by local time, and again blazingly hot."

When we got to the Empress Hotel we found that too few rooms had been reserved for us. David made a scene, called for the Manager and dispatched me to ring up our travel agent, American Express, and complain, but fortunately before I had managed even to find their number the smiling reception clerk reappeared to say that everything had been arranged. We foregathered in the Outrigger Bar, where I rather gingerly sampled a mixture of rum and lime called a Waikiki Delight.

"Peter had already found out a restaurant for us to go to and had booked a table there for 9.30. I was rather dismayed to hear this as David, who had been reviving himself with whisky, was already in a very merry mood when he joined us in the bar, and I thought two hours drinking might prove disastrous. Fortunately we all started to feel hungry before then, so we strolled out into the night – which was hot and humid and full of brightly lit Chinese signs and washing hanging from every window of the skyscrapers of Kowloon – to the Kingfisher Restaurant . . . When we finally left there it was late and David was only narrowly diverted from going into the Grand Hotel instead of the Empress. He invited us all up to his penthouse room to drink his duty-free whisky. I didn't fancy the whisky, but tried some Bacardi instead, not being quite sure what it was. In fact it's white rum and I won't try it again!." I left the gathering when David started expatiating on the villainies of the French Centre and how he was going to squash their enquiries into PEN's financial situation."

The next day, Wednesday, 17 June, after a sightseeing trip to the Peak, we flew on to Taipei:

"Arrived at Taipei after an hour and twenty minutes, flying out of bright sunshine into thick cloud over the island. From beneath the cloud the landscape looked like a kindergarten model of a relief map with hills, then patches of cultivation and a river running in wide loops. We were met at the airport by a welcoming committee, were whipped through without any Customs formalities, had our baggage claimed for us, and were taken off to the Mandarin Hotel, which turned out to be near and very palatial in style. After time to rest and change and unpack we were entertained to dinner in a private room at the hotel by various distinguished members of the local PEN – all men except for our hostess, Nancy Ing, a very charming half-Chinese, half-American woman. One of my neighbours, Dr. Kang, told me he was a direct descendant of Confucius, but when I told the others this they said he must have been pulling my leg.

We started off with cups of green tea in an anteroom, then went to an inner room and sat round a circular table with a revolving centrepiece – the first and longest of many such meals. A small glass full of rice wine and a tumbler of Coca-Cola stood beside each place, and the rice wine was constantly replenished. I kept taking nervous swigs, not realising for some time that etiquette demanded that every time one drank any wine it should be a toast to some individual at the table, catching his eye and saying his name (this presented a problem because they were all called Chen or Chun or Shu or Chu and I couldn't remember which was which). Another favourite device was to drink to 'the new dish', and there were plenty of those. We seemed to get through about seventeen courses. On the whole they were delicious, though there were some odd mixtures like small melons filled with chicken soup, and soup cropped up at odd intervals throughout the meal. I gave up chopsticks early on and used a fork. After dinner we adjourned to Peter's room, where the others imbibed their duty-free Scotch and I drank guava nectar."

Perhaps this is the moment to say that everyone in our party except me was a hardened whisky-bibber and since, in the course of our Far Eastern tour we passed through so many airports, at each of which the others each bought a duty-free bottle, some of them, particularly David and Kate, tended to get quite sloshed, and therefore argumentative, at our bedroom drinks parties. Since I did not like whisky in those days, and had evidently discovered that rum was not a good substitute, I took to non-alcoholic drinks. It must have been rather irritating for the others to have me sitting primly in a corner sipping fruit juice while they argued, but they treated me with kindly tolerance as the youngest and most inexperienced member of the party.

"THURSDAY, 18 JUNE
Had to get up early to have breakfast at 8 o'clock with all the other delegates in the Hall of Long Life at the invitation of some local notability who – as turned out to be usual – made us a long speech of welcome. This was a Western breakfast, prefaced by a delicious glass of orange juice. Liz and I sat with Virginia Cox Balmaceda – the fadedly glamorous Chilean delegate. At 9 o'clock we went by bus to the Airport and were taken on a short flight to Hualien on the East coast and were driven from there up the magnificent Taroko Gorge and given lunch at the Tien Hsiang Lodge up in the mountains. This was a most spectacular drive as the road (the East-West Highway) has been blasted out of the side of the gorge with sheer cliff above and below it and frequent tunnels and bridges. We made several stops – one to visit a charming temple by a spring in memory of the four hundred or more ex-servicemen who lost their lives in building the road, and one by a stretch of cliff riddled with holes where swallows built their nests. We asked what other wild life there was, and were told monkeys and deer, but saw none. Lunch was a slightly trying meal because Claude des Presles (Treasurer of French PEN) came and sat himself beside me and paid me various barbed compliments in French and English and made me even more self-conscious than usual about my chopstick technique.

After lunch (with more speeches) we were driven back down into the plain and taken to see a settlement of the aboriginal people of Taiwan (a type of Polynesians), where a band of girls, brightly decked with beads and feathers, danced for us, accompanied by one girl singing and another beating with a stick on a hollow log. They gave us a programme on which the last item read ominously: 'Let's All Join In The Dance'. Sure enough David and various other men were selected, decked out with crowns and robes and garlands, and first chaired round the dance floor by six girls and then made to dance in a circle. As Liz remarked, David, who was far too large for his crown, looked like a large boiled egg in a small egg-cup.

After the girls had waved us goodbye we were taken to see round a marble factory, where they cut and shaped locally quarried marble, and were each given a paper-weight as a souvenir."

On our return to Taipei we were entertained to dinner at the Armed Forces Officers' Club by Mr. Chen Yu-chin, Chairman of the National Council of Literature and Arts, who had been one of my neighbours at dinner on the first night. Liz and I sat opposite some charming young people who were members of the local PEN Working Committee. One of them, a good-looking boy of about eighteen, told us that he was very anxious to have a correct English pronunciation rather than the American English which is more common in Taiwan. He asked us how to pronounce such words as "schedule" and whether Peter O'Toole or Richard Burton spoke better English.

"FRIDAY, 19 JUNE
We were once more entertained to breakfast at 8 o'clock – this time a typical Chinese breakfast given by the Director of the Taiwan Tourism Bureau. I sat between Peter and one of our Chinese hosts. The food was interesting but very thirst-making as it chiefly consisted of various different sorts of fritters. There was also a piece of pastry in the shape of a fish, stuffed with bean paste. The drink was some kind of bean milk, sweetened and drunk from bowls . . . We were taken out to a luncheon at the Ambassador Hotel, given by the President of the Anti-Communist League. Among the speakers were an apparently very distinguished Chinese painter called Tang, who had rimless spectacles, a venerable beard and wore a nightgown, and Sophia Wadia (the Founder and President of the All-India PEN Centre, a Belgian woman who had married a Parsee and become more Indian than the Indians). Mr. Tang's speech was very long and rambling and had to be translated from the Chinese, so I was more than half asleep when Madame Wadia started in. She made a very histrionic speech based on the inscription by the spring in the shrine we had visited the previous day: 'Listen to the song of the waters and Spring will be eternal'. David's face was a study!"

The dinner that evening, given by His Excellency C. K. Yen, Vice-President of the Republic, at the Grand Hotel, was excellent, only interrupted by a very mild earth tremor – a foretaste of things to come. David decreed that, since our host was the Vice-President, our dress should be formal, so he appeared resplendent in a dinner jacket and Liz and I in evening dresses. I was very embarrassed to find myself so over-dressed in comparison to most of the other delegates.

"We had drinks in Peter's room afterwards and when we separated for the night we all went to the lifts together. David pressed the button and the lift door opened rather too quickly for a young Chinese couple who were revealed in close embrace inside the lift, and sprang apart giggling in embarrassment. David looked at them benevolently over his spectacles, pressed the buttons for our various floors, and said: 'Five, six, seven. And then we leave you.'

The next day we were taken to see the wonders of the Palace Museum, which is stocked with all the treasures which Chiang Kai-shek and his followers brought with them from the Mainland. I particularly admired the twelfth century landscape paintings and the porcelain and jade. Lin Yutang, the benign and scholarly President of the PEN Centre, entertained us to a buffet lunch at which he regaled us with details of the private life of Mr. Tang, the painter. Apparently Mr. Tang had built himself a fabulous mansion in Brazil and had six concubines until they got bored with Brazil. Now he was down to one concubine.

"In the afternoon the main event of the day took place. Dressed in our best, we were driven out to the President's reception hall (not the same as his residence) on a hill outside the city. We arrived well in advance of the other delegates and so got good positions in the red-carpeted reception hall, where couches and chairs were arranged in semi-circles to face the central aisle. David was conducted to a seat by the central couch where Chiang Kai-shek and Madame were to sit, and Dr. Rahnema (President of the Iranian Centre) caused a stir among the protocol section by insisting on sitting there too although he was not listed among the V.I.P.'s. After we had all been offered a choice of tea, orange juice or Coca-Cola, much to Kate's disgust since she had hoped for something stronger, there was a stir among the military and officials clustered round the doorway and the President and Madame entered arm in arm, bowing and smiling graciously from side to side. He looked old (he is eighty-three) and benevolent; she is seventy, but still looks beautiful, with masses of black hair. She was wearing a long white dress. We then all sat down and were given little iced cakes to eat. I made stilted conversation to Pham Viet-Tuyen, from Vietnam, whose

English is not nearly as good as his French. 'What sort of literature write you?' he enquired charmingly.

SUNDAY, 21 JUNE
Breakfasted fairly late in company with Kate, then packed and she and I set out for a walk as we had not had a chance to explore anywhere on foot. This was not a great success as it was bakingly hot and there was really nowhere to walk to as round about the Mandarin Hotel there is nothing but a few shops and apartment blocks dotted in the midst of scruffy patches of green vegetation. We turned back after we had walked two or three blocks and she treated me to an orange juice in the hotel coffee bar and a long story about how Mary Treadgold and Philip Toynbee lost their shoes at Kyoto during a rain storm at the 1957 Japanese Congress, and I told her about the American woman I had got into conversation with in the hotel lobby who had asked me whether Ted Heath was 'communistic'."

Our next port of call, on the way to Seoul, was Tokyo. All these flights were a great trial to Kate, who had a phobia about flying. Peter, who had trained as an R.A.F. pilot before the Second World War, tried to help during take-off by telling her exactly what the pilot was doing at each moment, but that only infuriated her. I sat next to her on most of the flights, and, because of her deafness, had to relay the pilot's announcements to her. As we circled Tokyo airport prior to landing, the pilot said over the intercom, with what seemed to me to be disastrous clarity: "We can't land yet because there's been a crash on the runway." "What's that?" said Kate, "What did he say?" With unusual quickness of invention, I replied: "He says we're having to wait to land because there's a bit of a crush on the runway". This seemed to satisfy Kate at the time, but afterwards she hotly denied that she had been deceived even for a moment.

"MONDAY, 22 JUNE
All of us except Peter set out on foot in the rain to explore Tokyo. After walking for some time in what we hoped was the direction of the Imperial Palace, David and Kate went into a building which looked like a post office to enquire our whereabouts. The people there said 'Sightseeing?' and forthwith produced a notice in English which said that visitors were only allowed in the building with the permission of an M.P., from which we gathered that this was not a post office, but the Parliament Building. From there, by diligent and lucky map-reading on my part, we found our way to the Imperial

Hotel, getting a view of the Palace grounds and the lake on the way. We all had drinks in the bar at the Imperial and then got a taxi back to the New Japan, where we were staying. In the afternoon we met Edward Seidensticker, Kawabata's translator, for a drink. He is a pleasant, middle-aged American academic. He is a great expert on all oriental languages and told us that Chinese is a very profane language, Japanese not nearly so much so, but it is very easy to be insulting by being over-polite. There are apparently about fifty different ways of saying 'you', each with a different significance."

Arriving in Seoul a week before the start of the Congress we embarked on a packed programme of sight-seeing, socialising and being given the red carpet treatment. First we were entertained to a welcome party by the Organising Committee for the Congress at which I was at once captivated by the Koreans' informality and infectious sense of humour:

"One of the men came up to me and said: 'You look very passionate'. His friend – who must have caught a fleeting expression of surprise on my face – giggled and asked whether this was the correct thing to say to a lady. I replied cautiously that I thought his friend had possibly got the wrong word.

WEDNESDAY, 24 JUNE
We were taken by Miss Moh and Dr. Kwack to be presented to the Prime Minister, Chung Il-Kwan. He received us very courteously and told us in excellent English how he had been in command of the forces next to the Gloucesters during the Korean War. He also showed us the cabinet room and gave us an outline of their system of government. My attention was slightly distracted by the fact that one of my self-supporting stockings had ceased to be self-supporting and was threatening to fall down round my ankle. We then had a brief interview with Minister Tsin, the Minister of Culture, who spoke through an interpreter entirely about the weather.

THURSDAY, 25 JUNE
Helped Kate with a press interview at which a very charming young girl tried – with great lack of success – to get the feminine viewpoint on English women writers. As Kate had given an interview the previous day to *The Korean Times* in which she had been reported as saying that she had been living in Japan for a year, and had apparently (according to the accompanying

photograph) grown a beard during that time, heaven knows how this interview will turn out.

As a car had been put at our disposal, we decided to go for a drive to see something of the city, but no sooner had we set out than a thunderstorm broke, with torrential rain, so we had to turn back. This was just as well as it turned out because Miss Moh had made a lunch appointment for us with Mrs. Kim, the wife of a wealthy businessman (Chairman of the I.P.A.), and we were due to leave the hotel at 12 o'clock, not, as I had thought, at 12.30. What should have been a forty minute drive in fact took three hours. Miss Moh, David and Peter went ahead in one car, while Kate, Liz and I followed in our official car, but we soon lost sight of them as all the streets became torrents of muddy yellow water and the traffic snarled up into apparently indissoluble blocks. We thought that at any moment our car's' engine would stall and never start again. The pedestrians had a very poor time as they were paddling about – sometimes knee-deep or more – among the traffic, which was even blocked solid on the pavements. Our driver, stuck with three foreigners and unable to communicate with them, showed great self-control and enterprise in worming his way in and out of the other traffic.

We finally, after driving through a rather slummy area, reached the Kims' splendid house at the foot of the mountains at about 3.30. We drove through a gateway with two servants bowing to us and up to an undercover entrance, where we were ushered in by a major-domo. We left our shoes outside in the approved fashion and donned slippers. I took a very splendid red and silver pair, but Liz, who came in last, was faced with a lady's size three pair, so had to go without. Mrs. Kim, who was entertaining us in the absence of her husband, was a beautiful, rather shy, woman of about forty, dressed in traditional garb, and her house showed signs of great wealth. The original house was several hundred years old, with a fascinating pagoda-style roof. Built onto this were various modern extensions looking like sun-lounges. The whole thing was on an open plan, with beautiful furniture and ornaments wherever you looked and not a thing out of place. As Liz said, it was rather too like a hotel, with a sort of reception desk in the hall with a telephone on it, and a cocktail bar in the sitting-room. Outside there was a beautiful lawn with landscaped miniature trees in front and a rockery with an artificial waterfall splashing down into a pool behind.

There was no sign in our entertainment that we had arrived three hours late for lunch. We were served by a smiling manservant with any sort of drink we cared to name, and then conducted to a table beautifully set with silver (including silver chopsticks) and crystal glasses. After a Korean-style meal coffee was served in gold-encrusted cups and accompanied by liqueurs. We were supposed to visit the Kims' Korean-style guest house on our way back, but Liz, Peter and I got into the official car and were whisked straight back to the hotel. Fortunately all the traffic had cleared away and the journey back only took us forty minutes."

The next evening Miss Moh gave a dinner party in her house, which was on the top of a hill on the edge of the city, near some old burial mounds. We started off with drinks on the lawn, which was delightful. At dinner we were all seated on very low seats, in the Korean fashion, with nowhere – so it seemed to me – to put our legs. The British Ambassador, Nigel Trench, who was seated opposite me, was very tall and elegant, but managed diplomatically to stow his legs away in some graceful and inconspicuous way. My knees kept appearing above table level, not unobserved by Miss Moh, who commented disapprovingly from the head of the table on this breach of manners. I was also closely observed by my neighbour Dr. Bok-Nok Kwack, the Secretary of Korean PEN, who took a poor view of my technique with chopsticks (which I was by now rather proud of) and disconcerted me by saying in the middle of the meal: "If you're really hungry, Miss Paterson, you could use a spoon."

This was not the first time we had met the British Ambassador. We had been to call on him on our arrival in Seoul and had been dismayed when our taxi driver had had to stop and ask someone where the British Embassy was. It turned out to be very small and insignificant and tucked away in a corner. Perhaps it was a reaction to the discovery of Britain's lost status in this far corner of Asia that caused David to address the Ambassador as "Your Excellency" in every other sentence, much to that modest man's embarrassment.

"SATURDAY, 27 JUNE
David went out to the airport, with the French Ambassador, to meet Pierre Emmanuel, who arrived at 11.50 a.m. – in a cheerful mood fortunately. (This is a reference to Emmanuel's manic depressive temperament.) We opened up the International Secretariat office on the first floor of the hotel and I spent most of the day in there typing various conference papers. Meanwhile all the delegates were arriving. In the evening Kate, Peter and I went, with a lot of the other delegates, in a bus to Inchon, the port on the West coast, to a reception given there by the Korean

Women Writers (of whom there seem to be many). The drive (of about twenty miles) was very pleasant as the sun was shining and we were able to see something of the countryside – mostly rice paddies, but also a few small hills and some villages, looking very picturesque with their low thatched roofs, but obviously pretty primitive inside. When we reached the Olympos Hotel at Inchon we were taken up to a room on the eighth floor with a fine view on both sides over the harbour. There we were warmly welcomed by several very charming Korean ladies, who were all touchingly grateful to us for coming, and were given drinks and very good snacks. We tucked into these, thinking, from previous experience, that this would be all the food we should get. But, not a bit of it, we were then made to line up at a counter and had our plates piled high with food. After dinner a plump and pleasant lady, who I gathered was a teacher of singing and was obviously a well-known performer, was prevailed upon to sing us some Korean folk songs, which she did with great verve. Then we were expected to dance, which, considering the proportion of men to women was about 1 to 10, was a little awkward. At last the bus came to get us back to Seoul before the midnight curfew. Got back to my room to find that a whole library of books and pamphlets on Korea had been delivered to me".

This was only the first of many such deliveries. Every evening when we returned to our hotel rooms it was to find a fresh present added to the pile already accumulated there: a set of records of Korean folk-songs given by the Minister of Culture, a jewel box from Miss Moh, a fan, a china plate, lengths of Korean silk, pictures . . . Eventually we had to have them all shipped home in a crate.

Miss Moh, who had been a heroine of the resistance against the Japanese, mistress of Krishna Menon, and co-founder with Mrs. Chun and Mrs. Cho of the Korean PEN Centre, was a very forceful and passionate character, before whom government ministers and ambassadors quailed. She took a great fancy to David's tall and handsome presence and enjoyed it when he opened the Ball with her. She turned to me in considerable irritation when he subsequently led the Chilean delegate, Virginia Cox Balmaceda, onto the floor and said: "Why is Mr. Carver dancing with Mrs. Chile?". Virginia Cox became "Mrs. Chile" to us henceforward, and Hyam Brezniak, the delegate from Sydney, with whom she had formed a Congress friendship, became "Mr. Australia".

Amongst the foreign participants the centre of interest for the South Korean press was Mira Mihelic, guest of honour from the Slovene

Centre. The Koreans had done their best to get delegates from the Communist Bloc to attend the Congress, but none of them had accepted, so they made much of the triumph of having a Yugoslav there, which Mira accepted with her customary grace and modesty. In the discussion of writers in prison, the case of Kim Chi-Ha, recently arrested for his poem *The Five Bandits*, which satirised the leaders of the government, was raised for the first of many times, and the Korean PEN agreed to work for his release in spite of their feeling that the poem constituted a political act. The literary discussions, on the theme of "Humour in Literature – East and West', resulted in a thick book, but very little humour.

David had to take an even more than usually prominent part in this Congress because the International President, Pierre Emmanuel, having been greeted on his arrival in Seoul by David and the French Ambassador and taken off to dinner at the French Embassy, had nearly died in the night from a perforated ulcer, had to be rushed to the American Hospital, and so could take no part in the Congress. I think the Korean PEN felt that they had not got their money's worth out of his first-class fare from Paris to Seoul. Miss Moh certainly blamed it all on the French Ambassador.

"SUNDAY, 28 JUNE
Fortunately I got up early, but even so I was in the bath when the phone rang about 7.30. This was Liz, starting with the ominous words 'The whole thing is falling apart like a pack of cards'" She then broke the news about Pierre Emmanuel.

"Miss Moh had been up since crack of dawn, but there was great delay in getting a doctor and Pierre Emmanuel had refused to go into hospital. I hastily got dressed and had my breakfast and went along to David's room, to find him in a state of undress, but reasonably calm. A doctor and nurse arrived and were taken along to Pierre Emmanuel's room, and Robert Goffin (the peppery lawyer who was President of the Francophone Belgian Centre and the only International Vice-President who had made the journey to Seoul) was alerted that he would have to chair the Executive. He did this well and we got through the business fairly smoothly, with only one eruption from the Israeli delegation (no doubt in reply to some challenge from the Lebanese delegate, Camille Aboussouan, about censorship of Palestinians).

After the meeting we went up to David's room while Peter drafted a statement for the Press, and then I went down to the office to type it . . . Just managed to get changed in time to go to a reception given by Dr. Paik at Yung Bin Kwan (the State Guest House), a pleasant traditional style building on top of a hill. This was said to be a reception and dinner, but was in fact only drinks and a buffet, so you never can tell! We left in rather a hurry as Mrs. Lyung told me that they had been appealing for blood donors over the radio for Pierre Emmanuel as he is rhesus negative. The poor man has now had five haemorrhages and been taken to the American Military Hospital.

MONDAY, 29 JUNE
Started the day with many fruitless attempts to get in touch with the American Military Hospital to find out how Pierre Emmanuel was. At first I found I was dialling the wrong number, and then the nurse I got on to was ultra-correct and refused to give me any information.

The Opening Ceremony, from 10.00 to 11.00 , went off well, and Goffin delivered an excellent piece of oratory in place of Pierre."

In the afternoon we went from a sightseeing tour of Seoul to a tea-party at the British Embassy to a reception given by President Park and Madame Park at their official residence. I cannot imagine how we kept up this frantic pace. It's no wonder that my diary quite often records that I retired to bed early with a headache or a tummy bug. On the President's reception I commented:

"This was a very democratic affair, where the President and Madame Park, the Prime Minister and the Mayor of Seoul circulated freely among their guests – so freely in fact that the President, who is a very small man, was practically trampled underfoot by us clumsy occidentals. Madame Park was tall and graceful and very beautiful.

TUESDAY, 30 JUNE
The first literary session, on 'Regional Characteristics of Humour' was very well chaired by Donald Keene, though the contributions varied a great deal in standard . . . We were given lunch by the Minister of Education at the Tower Hotel at which I sat next to Camille Aboussouan, a very polished cosmopolitan with a dry sense of humour, who confided in me that he found the Korean women's traditional dress very frustrating to his 'low Mediterranean taste'.

WEDNESDAY, 1 JULY
John Updike gave a very good lecture on "Humour in Fiction", in the course of which: he read aloud and then discussed passages from *Don Quixote*, Voltaire's *Candide* and *Huckleberry Finn*.

Then followed a literary session on 'Function of Humour In Contermporary Society', chaired by Goffin. At this Kate gave the first paper and spoke for just over the stipulated seven minutes, with the result that Goffin, in his usual arbitrary fashion, interrupted her three sentences before the end – not a popular move!"

On the following day (2 July) Kate and I were invited by Mrs. Hahn Moon-sook to a lunch party in honour of John Updike. Mrs. Hahn had been one of the Korean delegates to the Menton Congress the previous year and the luncheon invitation was my reward for supplying her with antihistamine pills when she was suffering from an allergic reaction on the trip to Monte Carlo. She turned out to be the wife of a banker and had a charming, fifty-year-old house built in the traditional style round a small courtyard with flowers and a pond. John Updike (who was there with his daughter Elizabeth) was very unassuming and friendly. There was a photographer in attendance and we were each given a packet of photographs when we left, so I have pictures of John Updike and me sitting side by side on a low seat, grappling rather inexpertly with our chopsticks. I also have a ring set with a very large topaz, which I've never felt able to wear. Each of the women guests were given one, and I think each of the men was given a tie-pin, also set with a topaz. I can't imagine that John Updike ever wore his tie-pin either.

Because of Mrs. Hahn's sumptuous hospitality I arrived late at the Women's University of Eowa to witness David being awarded an honorary doctorate in literature. Embarrassingly I was shown to a seat in the front row of the auditorium, where I came under the observation of the British Ambassador, who said to me at the tea-party which followed that I must have had a very good lunch as I appeared to be asleep half the time. I was also observed by David, who said that he could see me trying not to laugh, which was nearer the truth. The ceremony of awarding David's doctorate was performed by the very small lady Principal of the University, Dr. Louisa Yim, who was half his height and so had to climb on to a sort of mounting block in order to be able to invest him with his doctoral hood. He then had a magnificent garland strung round his neck, so that I was irresistibly reminded of the lines addressed to Bunthorne by the chorus in the Gilbert and Sullivan opera *Patience*:

> 'Oh Poet now say you
> Why thus they array you
> Oh tell us, we pray you,
> What is it you've done?'

David took his degree very seriously and expected to be addressed as Dr. Carver thereafter. He was not at all amused, therefore, when Peter teased him on the way back from the university by putting his head into our taxi and asking whether there was a doctor in the car.

"That evening we were taken in Miss Moh's car, with the usual outriders, to Sun Woon Kak, a four-star restaurant in a beautiful situation right up in the mountains beside a stream. We had drinks outside on the lawn with a wonderful smell of pine trees and mountains in the air, and were then conducted indoors to a Korean-style party, at which we were served by kisaeng (the Korean equivalent of geishas). These were very charming girls, but we females felt a bit de trop. We were entertained by some folk-singing and then danced. David and the rest of our party left before the end at the invitation of Mr. S. Y. Kim, our host for the evening, to visit his house once again which was very close by. This turned out to be a very embarrassing end to the evening. Both David and Mr. Kim got extremely drunk; as did also an American Korean who had attached himself to our party and divided his time between (figuratively) licking Mr. Kim's boots and (literally) pawing Kate and me. Kate, who was also a bit high, worked herself up into a fury about David's condition and the fact that we probably wouldn't get back to our hotel before the curfew. In the circumstances it was only the sight of the waterfall illuminated and the gentle charm of Mrs. Kim which saved the day. We finally got away at 11.30 (Peter, Kate and I in one car, David and Liz in the other) and got back to the hotel on the dot of midnight. Our driver seemed quite unbothered, so presumably Mr. S. Y. Kim is above the law."

The previous day we had been taken, under American military escort, to the 38th parallel at Panmunjom, from where we could see across the Bridge of No Return into North Korea. The view of the mountains was magnificent and all seemed peaceful, but we were given strict instructions not on any account to reply to any insults from the North Korean guards or to enter any building painted white. We were also told, as we were being driven back to the U.S. Army base that their jeeps were often ambushed on this road. David was unamused by Peter's suggestion that it would be a good story for the newspapers and good publicity for PEN if the International Secretary were to be kidnapped by the North Koreans!

"FRIDAY, 3 JULY
Last day of the official Congress proceedings. I missed the final
literary session, which was on 'Humour As A Means of
Furthering International Understanding', with Edward Blishen in
the Chair, because I had to type David's speech for the Closing
Ceremony that afternoon ... The final event of the Congress was
the buffet and ball given by Miss Moh on the top floor of the
KAL building. I felt I must at least put in an appearance at this,
wearing my evening dress, but felt a bit out on a limb as Kate
had cried off because of back-ache and Liz at the last moment
bust the zip on her only evening dress and so couldn't come. I
was relieved to see that there were several other ladies wearing
long dresses, including Elizabeth Updike and Karna Dannevig
(the Norwegian delegate) and mine was much admired by In-sob
Zong and Mr. Kwack (So-gin), who came up to me and said
'You look so gracious'. David opened the ball with Miss Moh
and I was just wondering whether I should be able to get out of
dancing when my neighbour at dinner, Yang Wan-da, saying that
he was too small to dance with me himself, summoned Dr.
Chang, who is rather tall for a Korean, and we had to take the
floor together. Dr. Chang is a pleasant man whom I had met at
Hahn Moon-sook's lunch party. He is a professor of English
Literature at one of the Seoul universities and an even worse
dancer than me. He was, however, a dancer of some
determination. He seized me round the waist and set off at great
speed and with a complete disregard of anyone else on the dance
floor or what tune the band happened to be playing. After that it
was a relief to dance with John Foot (the bluff delegate from
New Zealand), who was really too far gone to do more than
stand on the dance floor with me. I was then claimed again by
Dr. Chang, who obviously regarded me as his social duty for the
evening, until Charles Flood (Charles Bracelen Flood, the
President of American PEN) cut in and claimed me from him.
After Charles had 'walked me back to my seat', it was getting on
for 9.30 and I wondered how I could decently make an exit.
Fortunately I was able to catch Peter and he kindly escorted me
back to the hotel on foot before going back to the ball. I was
then able to do all my packing, have a leisurely bath and get to
bed in good time before our early start the next day for the
post-Congress tour ...

SATURDAY, 4 JULY

Set off at 8.00 in the pouring rain for Seoul railway station, where we boarded a very comfortable train and set off for a five-hour journey to Pusan on the south-east coast. The weather cleared up as we went along, so that we got a good view of the really superb countryside – mountains and valleys and rice paddies, with the occasional thatch-roofed village. Pusan itself, where we arrived about lunchtime, is a messy industrial port, and the hotel, to which we were taken by a half-hour bus ride, was a great disappointment. Our guide told us on the way there that the beach rivalled Miami Beach with its crystalline sand and clear water, but when we arrived we found a long stretch of dirty grey sand with a row of flimsy shacks behind it crowded with people and loud with music blaring from microphones. There were quite big waves breaking, but the sea was a distinctly muddy colour and very unattractive for bathing. The hotel was not, of course, anywhere near the luxurious standard of the Chosun and Liz and I shared a room with a sideways view of the sea and a large factory chimney in the foreground. A situation reminiscent of last year's post-Congress tour to Corsica arose since about twenty Japanese delegates turned up without having registered and had to be parked out wherever there was a space, so one scarcely dared to leave one's room unoccupied for fear of coming back and finding a Japanese gentleman in possession.

We had a very late and very indifferent lunch, and then Liz, Kate and I set out for a stroll along the beach, paddling in the edge of the sea – which was surprisingly cold. The only PEN delegate we saw bathing was Hsiung Shih-I (author of the play 'Lady Precious Stream' which had had a very successful run in the West End). When we first saw him in Taipei wearing his traditional nightgown and bangles and tiny dancing pumps, and supported by his daughter and niece, he gave the impression of being frail and elderly, but once away from Taiwan he brisked up considerably and in Pusan he disported himself in the waves for an hour, looking like a small, rotund porpoise.

In the evening we were given dinner by the Mayor of Pusan. This was rather inedible and wasn't helped by the fact that David had just seen a rat running out of the kitchen premises.

During the night there was a great storm of rain – the backlash of Typhoon Olga – which caused quite a lot of devastation in the area, and it was still pouring with rain when Miss Moh took us into Pusan in her car to shop for jewellery for David to take home to his wife Blanche. After David had successfully made some purchases, we went back to the hotel and had drinks in the Sky Lounge while Miss Moh kept us entertained with her view of the character of In-sob Zong (which was not flattering) and a description of how the Congress preparations had been made. Whenever she went into the office, she said she would find the people working there 'exploding and typing'.

SATURDAY, 5 JULY
We woke to find that it had rained itself out and looked like being a fine day . . .We crammed into buses and went first to the United Nations cemetery near Pusan, where the dead soldiers from the Korean War are buried in groups according to their countries. This is a very moving sight. Each plot of grass has the flag of its country flying over it and rows of small square tablets with just the name and age of the dead man and either a cross or a crescent. There seemed to be more Turks buried there than any other nation. Everyone went to the plot where their own countrymen were buried, and I came across John Foot standing by the New Zealand graves. 'These are mostly artillerymen', he said, 'And it'll be the same in Vietnam.'

We drove on, feeling sobered, and I got into conversation with my neighbour, a very charming little Vietnamese called Le Van Hoan, who spoke excellent English. He gave me some idea of what the Vietnam War feels like to the Vietnamese. I asked him about the rice paddies we were driving through, and he said that in Vietnam too they used to grow a lot of rice and export much of it, but now, because of defoliation, nothing would grow and they had to buy rice from other countries. We were taken to visit a new factory at Usan making fertiliser and he commented that they could not build anything like that in Vietnam because infiltrators would come and blow it up. 'We are between the hammer and the anvil,' he said. He told me he had ten children, one of them a girl of about 20 who had got cut off in North Vietnam and of whom they had heard no news since 1954.

After lunch at Kyongju, we were taken to a nearby temple of the Silla dynasty called Pulguksa. This was very beautiful – courtyards and pagodas elaborately decorated with dragon heads, and altars attended by Buddhist monks making their monotonous chant and beating their wooden rattles. From here we piled into a fleet of thirty taxis and wound our way up a very rough mud track with a hundred and eighty-three bends, each more slippery than the last, high into the mountains to see the great stone Buddha in the cave in the mountainside at Sukkaram. From here we had the most magnificent view I have ever seen, looking east over mountains and rivers to a distant glimpse of the Japan Sea. At sunrise, apparently, the light is reflected from the Sea onto the forehead of the Buddha."

When I revisited the shrine after the 1988 Seoul Congress a glass screen had been erected at the mouth of the cave to protect the statue from pollution, but in 1970 it was possible to walk right round it and to light a candle at its feet. I found myself lighting my candle beside Camille Aboussouan, his running battle with the Israeli delegates temporarily forgotten.

6

The following day David and the rest of us left Seoul on the next leg of our journey, to Manila, where we were to discuss with Frankie Jose, the ebullient Secretary of the Philippine PEN Centre, plans for a Congress in Manila in 1972 under the patronage of Imelda Marcos, who, at that time, two years before martial law was declared in The Philippines, saw herself as a patroness of the arts.

The morning after our arrival in Manila we were summoned to Malacanang Palace to be presented to Madame Marcos.

"She is a very good-looking woman, probably in her late thirties, with masses of dark hair, and, while we sat round on gilt chairs with appreciative social smiles, told us about her twelve-year-old son, who is going to be educated in England. She also gave her approval to the idea that the 1972 Congress should be held in Manila, and quite obviously what she says goes. (As Dr. Roces [the President of Philippine PEN], said afterwards apropos of getting money for the Congress: 'The First Lady will twist their arms!'). She then focussed her attention on our plans."

Having heard what our hosts intended for us, she turned to us and asked what we would really like to do. Peter, with his usual lack of bashfulness, said that we should like to go and lie on a beach somewhere to recover from the exhaustion of the Congress. She smiled and said: "I think that can be arranged." After this my memories seem to verge on fantasy, but are confirmed by my diary. Madame Marcos clicked her fingers and had a telephone brought to her on a silver salver and proceeded to make it clear to the wife of the Minister of Defence that she was expected to be delighted to lend us her beach house at Batangas for the night. Madame Marcos then sent us away to have lunch and fetch our night things and swimsuits. When we returned there were two helicopters and several armed guards awaiting us on the palace lawn. Kate immediately said that nothing would induce her to travel by helicopter, whereupon the palace aides said that they would lay on a minibus just for her.

The rest of us climbed into the helicopters, which took off and whirred, like giant insects, southwards over the whole spread of islands which make up The Philippines. I had never been in a helicopter before and found it thrilling, a bird's eye view without any of the vertigo which

I usually feel at looking down from a high place. Eventually we swooped down, in formation, and landed on a palm-fringed, sandy beach, with no habitations in sight except for our beach house, which was a simple thatched structure, with one bedroom wing for the men, another for the women, and a large, hexagonal, open-sided patio, with a splendid selection of basket chairs, swinging seats and lounging couches. When the helicopters had taken off again there was absolute peace. Nothing was visible out to sea except for one small crescent island; the nearest fishing village was out of sight round the point.

"After a blissful swim in the tepid sea, we sat around in our bathing costumes and watched the sun set. We also watched one of the locals trying to harness a refractory ox to a cart loaded with stones. As the ox was only led by a ring through its nose, the man seemed to have very little control over it, and finally had to take it away and feed it, after which it was very docile. About 7.00 Kate arrived with two more guards, having had a very dangerous ride through guerrilla-infested country, which was why her escorts wore revolvers carelessly tucked into their belts. Much later on, when we were all practically asleep, the fishing boats came in and some beautiful fresh fried fish was produced for us to eat with our fingers."

Kate had quite enjoyed her drive until about halfway through the mountains, when one of the guards accompanying her had said: "Aren't you nervous, Miss Nott?" "Nervous? Certainly not!" she had said, "Why should I be nervous?". He had then told her that it was at this point that the guerrillas usually attacked passing traffic. Luckily this time they did not do so, but when the time came for us to leave Kate meekly accepted a helicopter ride.

THURSDAY, 9 JULY
"I was sleeping in a top bunk over Kate and, as I had left my watch in my handbag, I had no idea what the time was when I woke up. When I had climbed down I found it was just before 6.00, but as I was wide awake I decided to get into my bathing costume and have a swim. When I went out onto the patio I found David sitting there in his dressing-gown chatting to the boys, who had apparently been sleeping there all night, keeping armed watch turn and turn about. 'We look after you', they said. They were also keeping a close eye on who slept where, Peter said. He went down to the beach in the middle of the night to see if he could see the Southern Cross, and was closely watched on his return to see where he went.

As soon as I appeared I was presented with a cup of hot water and a tray of Nescafé, sugar and tinned milk. Even this concoction tasted very good when drunk early in the morning by a tropical sea.

When David had got into his bathing trunks we went for a swim and found the water refreshingly cool – even pleasanter than the night before. Peter joined us later and when we came out we found breakfast awaiting us in the shape of fried eggs and bread – the boys were very apologetic that there was no butter. After breakfast Kate was prevailed upon to enter the sea wearing Liz's bathing costume, which she split in three places.

After lazing around for half the morning, David, Peter, Leo and I were taken for an excursion round the bay in an outrigger with an inboard motor. This was fascinating – beautiful clear green water. As we were coming back we saw the two helicopters flying in in close formation to land, one behind the other, on the beach.

After the crews had had time for rest and refreshment, we climbed aboard and set off to return to Manila. This time David, Leo and I were in the second helicopter along with one of Kate's escorts, a man called Ramon, who had had more than his share of the San Miguel beer and kept shouting unintelligible commentaries on the landscape we were passing over. In the middle of the flight he tapped David on the shoulder, pointed to me and said: 'And who is this lady?', obviously having concluded that I was David's mistress. He then seized my hand and formally introduced himself. We landed on the same lawn we had taken off from the previous day and were transported by taxi – feeling very hot, sticky and dirty – back to our hotel.

After I had had a shower and changed I found the others all drinking in Liz's room. This went on rather too long, as Kate and Peter started to tell David how PEN should be run, which he immediately took as a personal insult, and the party broke up in some disorder."

We stayed some days in Manila and were splendidly entertained by Frankie Jose, who gave a party in his bookshop for us, and tried to persuade us to extend our stay and visit Baguio – up in the mountains. David had become addicted to the life of a distinguished guest and wanted to take Frankie up on his offer, but the rest of us could not wait to get to our last stop on the way home, Ceylon (as Sri Lanka was still called in those days), and become ordinary tourists for a change. This might have led to friction, had it not been for a convenient earthquake.

SATURDAY, 11 JULY

"The longest and least enjoyable day of our trip. It started at
5.15 a.m. with a moderately severe earth tremor. This only lasted
seven seconds, but it felt a good deal longer. I had been woken
up just before it by the thunder, and was lying in bed when I
suddenly had the sensation as of being in a boat which was
rolling heavily and saw the overhead light swinging to and fro on
its cord. Peter says he heard the steel girders creaking, but I can't
say I noticed this. I wasn't in fact very frightened. I simply
thought 'This is it. I'm on the fourteenth floor so there's nothing
I can do about it. Perhaps it's better to be on the top rather than
underneath when the building collapses'. When the tremor
finished I got out of bed and put my dressing-gown on so as to
meet my fate with some decency. Then I went and looked out of
the window to see if there was going to be a tidal wave or any
other excitements, but life seemed to be going on normally, with
cars and pedestrians going about their business. There seemed to
be no noise coming from outside my door, so I concluded that
whatever it had been was over and I must have exaggerated it,
and I went back to bed and slept. Peter rang up later, just as I
was about to go down to breakfast, to see if I was all right, and I
found that my monumental calm had not been universal. David
had knocked on Kate's door ('To see if she was all right') and
she had rushed into his room in her negligée, shutting her door
key in her room. They had then rung Peter to ask him what they
should do and whether they should go downstairs. He had very
sensibly said: 'No, you don't want to get caught in the lift', so
they had started imbibing Scotch! When we saw Frankie later he
dismissed the whole thing with a laugh and said that if it had
been a bad earthquake all the books would have been shaken off
the shelves in his shop. There had been quite a bad earthquake in
April which had caused all the guests to run out of the Hilton in
their night attire because their bedroom walls had fallen down."

One fortunate result of the earthquake was that David suddenly
became very keen to get away from Manila and we were able to leave
the next day, as planned, for Ceylon.

Throughout our journeyings and many currency changes we had
indulged in complicated transactions to keep our finances in order,
so that for weeks after I got home I would find scribbles on the backs
of envelopes saying: "I owe Peter 1000 yen. I owe Liz 300 won. David
owes me 500 Philippine pesos . . . etc." Peter, in addition to his duties
as Press officer, took charge of our finances. When we landed at

Colombo Airport, he took me with him to change some money for the whole party. This money-changing mysteriously took place in a chemist's shop. I never discovered how he knew where to go or how legal the transaction was.

In Manila the heat had been humid; in Colombo it was dry and scorching. Our hotel, the Gall Face, which was an old-fashioned building with high-ceilinged rooms and echoing corridors, pleasurably cooled by fans, had a lawn running down to the Indian Ocean where we lounged in the shade of thatched umbrellas and had cool drinks brought to us by waiters wearing white sarongs and padding in bare feet. I lay back and imagined myself to be a memsahib under the Raj. What I had not taken into account was that the sun would burn even through a thatched umbrella, so, although I wore a sun hat, I left my arms and legs uncovered and they very swiftly turned an unbecoming and painful pink. Another mistake I made was when we went out to a restaurant for lunch. The rest of the party ordered lobster thermidor, whilst I, thinking it was the correct thing to do in Ceylon, foolishly ordered a "mild" chicken curry, which nearly took the roof off my mouth.

After I had slept this off, David summoned me to join him in a swim in the hotel pool. This was a salt-water pool with a palm-shaded terrace beside it with a notice saying "Beware of falling coconuts".

On our second day in Ceylon we hired an air-conditioned station wagon to take us up to Kandy. Soon after collecting us from our hotel, the driver, an elderly man called Mr. Akbar, discovered that the air conditioning was not working, so, instead of taking the road for Kandy, we headed for a garage in the back streets of Colombo to change our vehicle for another one. Kate became convinced that we were being kidnapped and kept poking Peter, who was sitting in the front seat beside the driver, and urging him to do something about it. Fortunately her fears proved unfounded and we eventually set out for Kandy.

"The first part of our route was very congested with traffic – bullock carts and old London buses, but when we got clear of them we made quite good speed. The road was palm-fringed almost the whole way and ran through a beautifully lush green countryside with frequent habitations.

Our first stop was to see Mr. Bandaranaike's tomb, where our driver picked various flowers to present to us, including frangipani and Buddha's seat (*sic*. Can this be right?). The scarlet canna lillies were blazing everywhere, and so were the poinseana and jacaranda trees.

After we had visited a tea factory (where we bought packets of Broken Orange Pekoe) and a rubber factory and paused to photograph our first elephant, the road started winding up into the hills, and Mr. Akbar pointed out Bible Rock. We arrived in Kandy just before 1.00 and were dropped for lunch at the Queen's Hotel – another remnant of the British Raj. During lunch it started to pour with rain, and it was still raining when we went up to the temple where Buddha's tooth is said to be enshrined. This was a wooden structure with faded paintwork – not particularly impressive compared with the splendid temple we saw at Kyongju.

Poor Peter had started feeling ill ever since drinking the milk of the king coconuts which the driver had bought for us by the roadside, so the rest of our trip was slightly curtailed. We were driven round the very magnificent Botanical Gardens and University, and shown the elephants having their bath in the river, and then made all speed back to Colombo, which we reached soon after 6.00. I was feeling exhausted and went straight to bed.

TUESDAY, 14 JULY

England, Home and Beauty. The airport bus picked us up at 8.45 after we had distributed a phenomenal number of tips, and we had a very rackety drive to the airport, which we didn't reach till 10.00. Peter was still feeling wretched, but fortunately managed to make it onto the plane, where he stretched out on a back seat and went to sleep. Our only stop was Teheran, which we reached after flying over a fascinating relief map of barren hills and river valleys – Afghanistan?"

It turned out that Peter had hepatitis and a high fever. I think that in any case by that time we had all had enough of travel and the monotony of tropical climates and were glad to get back to England and variable weather. It was a bonus to be met at the airport by Teresa, who had kindly driven out to collect us.

To Kevin FitzGerald   *Edinburgh*
Crossways, Chinnor, Oxon   *October 1970*

Dear Kevin,
Here we are practically back on home ground for the Edinburgh
Conference. We're staying in solid comfort at the George Hotel, where
I heard the hotel porter on the telephone firmly telling a tiresome
enquirer: "PEN stands for Poets, essaysists (sic) and novelists". Did
you know that we had these intruding essayists in our midst?! Much
Love, Elizabeth

Ronald Johnston, the adventure story writer, organised the Edinburgh
Conference and certainly did a good job. The preliminary announce-
ment, programme, dinner menus etc. were all ornamented with the
same picture – an old sepia print of the castle – and the whole meeting
was arranged with the same attention to detail, down to the final
banquet, at which every course was some typically Scottish delicacy,
including generous servings of Angus beef, and a singer entertained
us with Scottish songs, accompanying herself on the clarsach.

The meeting of the International Executive Committee was less
harmonious. Pierre Emmanuel was still out of action, so the chair was
taken by Rosamond Lehmann, whose quiet voice was compensated
for by the great respect in which her novels were held – particularly
by the French. In any case the majority of the delegates were male
and although she only retained the vestiges of her youthful beauty,
she still carried herself like a beautiful woman and had a magnetic
effect on the opposite sex. I had observed this enviously one day when
her car developed a puncture just as she was driving out of the yard
at Glebe House and two willing males immediately appeared as from
nowhere to change the wheel. When I told Kate this she commented
succinctly: "Rosamond is a girl who never has to carry her own
luggage".

Even Rosamond's graceful presence could not entirely prevent the
usual squabbles in the Committee and it was a relief when the meeting
was over and we were all taken by bus to see Sir Walter Scott's house,

Abbotsford, an outstanding example of the Scottish baronial style of architecture set in lovely Border scenery. We were welcomed charmingly by Patricia Maxwell-Scott, the elder of the two sisters, direct descendants of the novelist, who then still occupied part of the house. For some reason Peter was convinced (erroneously) that she had a title and he announced her to the coach party as Lady Maxwell-Scott. It was noticeable that this supposed contact with the aristocracy gave particular pleasure to the communist delegates!

It was just after our return from Edinburgh that Blanche Carver had a stroke which totally incapacitated her. She had been severely crippled with arthritis for several years before that, so I only knew her as a devoted background figure in David's life, gamely struggling around on crutches and never complaining of the pain she must have been suffering.

David had met her when, as an R.A.F. officer, he had served on the Duke of Windsor's staff in The Bahamas during the Second World War. Blanche, who was strikingly handsome, was then married to another member of the Duke's entourage, Sir Gerald Boles. When Sir Gerald was killed in a flying accident, Blanche was left a widow with a young son, Jeremy. I think David always regretted that when she married him she had to cease being Lady Boles and become plain Mrs. Carver. On our Far East tour, when he was slightly tipsy and wanting to impress our foreign hosts, he was occasionally heard to refer to her as "Lady Blanche", much to the irritated embarrassment of Liz Warner. After Blanche's stroke it fell to Liz to organise the complicated nursing care and housekeeping arrangements at the Carvers' house in Primrose Hill.

David was devoted to Blanche, but this did not prevent him when she could no longer go out, from accepting Mary Treadgold's invitations to dinners at her flat in Flood Street, where he was cosseted with delicious food and wine and the admiration which he enjoyed. He was also, although he pretended to us that he did it under sufferance, glad to accept Mary's invitation to spend a few days with her at the Trois Couronnes, a five star hotel at Vevey on Lake Geneva. Some years later, after David's death, Paul Theroux came to speak at a Glebe House meeting and I discovered, in conversation with him beforehand in the bar, that, on their journey to Vevey, David and Mary had shared a table with Paul in the dining-car on the train between Calais and Paris. Paul said that he had often speculated about the identity and relationship of the well-dressed elderly English couple whom he describes in his book "The Great Railway Bazaar" amongst the category: "gray-haired English couples who appeared to be embarking, with armloads of novels, on expensive literary adulteries":

"A waiter showed me to a table where a man and woman were tearing their bread rolls apart but not eating them . . .

'Angus was saying in The Times that he did research,' the man said. 'It just doesn't make sense.'

'I suppose Angus has to do research,' said the woman.

'Angus Wilson?' I said.

The man and woman looked at me. The woman was smiling, but the man gave me a rather unfriendly stare. He said,

'Graham Greene wouldn't have to do research.'

'Why not?' I said.

The man sighed. He said,

'He'd know it already.'

'I wish I could agree with you,' I said. 'But I read As If By Magic and I say to myself, "Now there's a real agronomist!" Then I read The Honorary Consul and the thirty-year-old doctor sounds an awful lot like a seventy-year-old novelist. Mind you, I think it's a good novel. I think you should read it. Wine?'

'No, thank you,' said the woman.

'Graham sent me a copy,' said the man. He spoke to the woman. 'Affectionately, Graham. That's what he wrote. It's in my bag.'

'He's a lovely man,' said the woman. 'I always like seeing Graham.'

There was a long silence . . .

'I love trains,' said the woman. 'Did you know the next carriage on is going to be attached to the Orient Express?'

'Yes,' I said. 'As a matter of fact –'

'Ridiculous,' said the man, addressing the small penciled square of paper the waiter had given him. He loaded the saucer with money and led the woman away without another glance at me."

That story rings very true. David never could bear competition.

8

To KEVIN FITZGERALD   *Portoroz, Slovenia*
Crossways, Chinnor, Oxon   *May 1971*

Dear Kevin,
We're on the Istrian Peninsula as guests of the four Yugoslav PEN
Centres. The meeting is called the Piran Conference, but is actually
taking place just round the corner from there in Portoroz, which has
the tourist hotels and a casino. The chief gambler in our party is
Simon Raven (who is here as the companion of Nina Bawden). We
escape to Piran whenever we can because it's a pretty little fishing
village with a very good restaurant. The whole coastline is beautiful.
Much love, Elizabeth

David had the annoying ability to knock back large quantities of drink
in the evening and appear none the worse for it the next morning.
One breakfast-time at Portoroz when several of us were sitting drooping round the table feeling rather fragile after whatever entertainment
had been laid on the night before, he breezed in, remarking exuber-
antly that a dip in the hotel pool with our fellow guests, most of
whom were German tourists of ample proportions, was like swimming
in a school of whales!

Pierre Emmanuel had recovered his health and presided at the
Portoroz meeting, but his manic depressive temperament made him
an unpredictable chairman. In those days International Presidents were
elected for a two-year term and could stand again for another two
years, so his first term of office was due to finish at the Dublin Congress
that September. The first day's meeting in Portoroz ended with a
shouting match between the Israeli and Lebanese delegates and, to
quote from my Minutes: "The discussion continued for some minutes
in an atmosphere of great disturbance, delegates shouting at one
another across the hall . . .". This caused Pierre Emmanuel to sweep
out, saying that, in the light of that discussion, he felt unable to accept
candidature for a second term. The next day, however, dawned bright
and sunny and he felt quite differently, telling the Committee that he

had changed his mind about standing again. Unfortunately for him, Bob den Doolaard (the redoubtable Dutch novelist, founder of the Foundation PEN Emergency Fund for getting money to the families of imprisoned writers) and others had got together the night before and persuaded Heinrich Böll (then President of the West German PEN) to stand. Hence the hotly contested election which was held in Dun Laoghaire – but more of that in a minute.

Other, more frivolous, memories of the Piran meeting: going by boat to picnic on an island and David's account of standing by the rail with Iván Boldizsár (President of Hungarian PEN) and suddenly losing Boldizsár's attention when the boat passed close to a nudist beach. And the last evening, when the waiters, bearing our dinner aloft, entered in procession to the strains of "Colonel Bogey". I shared a table with Charles Bracelen Flood, the rather serious-minded President of American PEN, and Alasdair Mackinnon, the translator, who was almost an honorary citizen of Slovenia because of his mastery of their language. In addition to his skill in languages, Alasdair was an accomplished mimic, and he reduced Charlie Flood and me to helpless laughter by telling us the entire story of *The Wizard of Oz*, reproducing all the voices, including the Munchkins. I expect the generous provision of slivovitz also had something to do with our condition. By the end of the dinner everyone was dancing, and I remember Bob den Doolaard bouncing towards me, in time to the music, with arms outstretched, and whirling me onto the floor.

*

Some time in 1971 Kathy Barazetti answered an advertisement we placed in the local paper for a book-keeper. She proved tougher and more competent than any of her predecessors, as well as having a panache which impressed David. She also introduced a friend of hers called Linda as manageress of the Glebe House Bar at lunchtime. Linda, an attractive redhead, was a very good organiser and produced reasonably priced and good lunches, which at least covered the expense of the cook and waitress, Marion and Marie, and even made a small profit, unlike the very delicious, but underpriced, dinners which Liz served up in the evenings at a heavy loss. Linda's father either was or had been in prison, and all three girls had chequered histories and dependent and disreputable male partners. (Marion was often found weeping into the potatoes as she peeled them at her partner Sonny's latest misdemeanour.) Marie's dyslexia made writing down orders difficult for her, but she was nevertheless a very competent waitress. As a keen observer of the English social scene, Gertie was amused by the contrast between Linda and her friends, whom she christened "the fringe girls", and the middle class, if not debbie, types whom PEN had tended to employ in the past. I think her preference was for the former.

9

To KEVIN FITZGERALD   *Dun Laoghaire*
Crossways, Chinnor, Oxon   *September*
                                                         1971

Dear Kevin,
I've been thinking of you ever since Katie and I arrived on Irish soil
– or at least when not stuffing delegates' folders and trying to cope
with the chaos caused by the electricians' strike. Desmond Clarke
assures us the strike will be over by the time everyone else arrives.
Although this is called the Dublin Congress, all the meetings are being
held in the Royal Marine Hotel here. Hope to get into Dublin one
evening. Much love, Elizabeth.

Katie and I went to the Dublin Congress in my mini. Assisted by
Gertie and Ian, we loaded it up in the Glebe House courtyard with
PEN documents, and our luggage and provisions for the journey, and
were only prevented at the last moment from driving off with Ian's
handbag, which had somehow got entangled with our luggage.

We crossed on the ferry from Holyhead to Dun Laoghaire and
arrived in Ireland, two days before the Congress was due to start, to
find it in the throes of an electricians' strike. This was arranged so
that all lighting and heating went off for a certain number of hours
each evening – I think it was from 6.00 to 10.00 In any case it threw
the kitchens of the Royal Marine Hotel into a state of total paralysis
so there was no dinner available on our first night. I offered to drive
Katie and Kate Nott round the streets of Dun Laoghaire in search of
fish and chips, but, just as we were about to set out, I caught sight,
at the candlelit reception counter, of some ladies from the Korean
delegation, exhausted from their marathon journey from Seoul and
evidently in difficulties. My first impulse was to escape before they
noticed me, but, remembering the superb hospitality we had received
from them the previous year, I felt obliged to abandon Katie and Kate
and go and see if I could help. It turned out that the problem was
that either the Koreans had not informed the Congress organisers that
they would be arriving early, or – more likely – the Irish had failed

to register the fact. In any case no rooms had been booked for them in the Royal Marine Hotel, which was the main conference hotel. The President of Irish PEN, Kenneth Deale, had gone to the airport to meet Pierre Emmanuel, and the Secretary, Desmond Clarke, lived the other side of Dublin and was inaccessible because, for some mysterious reason, the electricity strike had also put the telephone system out of action. Getting hungrier by the minute, I obtained from the receptionist a list of the other hotels in which the Korean ladies might have been booked, shepherded them, in a dazed state, into my mini, and drove round Dun Laoghaire spreading mystification in my wake as I assailed one candlelit reception desk after another, enquiring whether they had bookings for ladies with incomprehensible Korean names. The answer was that none of them had, so I whizzed the Koreans back to the Royal Marine Hotel to await the arrival of Kenneth Deale from the airport. He did eventually manage to get them into some expensive hotel outside Dun Laoghaire. That was not the end of my problems, however, because I found a furious Claude des Presles (Treasurer of French PEN) remonstrating with the unfortunate receptionist because no room had been reserved for him, although, as everyone knew, French PEN was entitled to an extra delegate for the Maison Internationale (the writers' house in Paris which they then ran). Fortunately, in my travels round Dun Laoghaire with the Korean ladies I had discovered a hotel which had a spare room, so I bundled Claude into my mini, drove him round there and deposited him, still fulminating. I returned to find that Katie, having given up all hope of fish and chips, had done some foraging in the hotel kitchens and produced tea and bread and butter. We were eating this ravenously when Kenneth Deale arrived. After watching us for a while, he said: "What a pity. If I'd known I'd have brought you a packet of biscuits"!

Fortunately the strike had finished by the time the main body of delegates arrived and, since Dun Laoghaire was bathed in warm September sunshine, the Congress was a great success. Katie and I took a more jaundiced view of it, since as soon as we arrived Desmond Clarke had dismissed all the staff who had been helping him with the Congress documents, on the assumption that we would take over. This meant that we passed a large part of the Congress in a basement, grappling with an inefficient duplicator which covered us with black ink, whilst we tried to produce hundreds of copies of all the literary papers. We did emerge, however, for the meetings of the International Executive Committee, and during one of the lunch-breaks I sat on the grass with Bob den Doolaard, who had given his usual flamboyant report on the work of the Foundation PEN Emergency Fund, an organisation which he had founded in The Netherlands and which did marvellous – but highly secret – work in smuggling money across forbidden frontiers to support the families of imprisoned writers. Bob loved the cloak and dagger aspect of the Foundation's work, particularly as it concerned the countries behind the Iron Curtain, for whose regimes he had nothing but loathing and contempt. As we ate our chicken salad in the September sunshine outside the Conference Centre he described to me with great relish an occasion when he had been taking money to writers' families in Czechoslovakia. He had been about to check in it at a hotel just outside Prague when he saw through the glass top of the door into the reception area two familiar and unwelcome figures: Heinz Kamnitzer and Henryk Keisch, who were checking out after representing the GDR PEN Centre at the funeral of some Party boss. If they had seen him they would have guessed his errand, so he immediately turned tail and went to a cinema. When he returned to the hotel he asked the receptionist whether his friends Professor Kamnitzer and Mr. Keisch were still in the hotel and expressed great disappointment when he heard that they had left.

I enjoyed this story and was startled when I made some reference to it later in the week and Bob rounded on me. "Who told you that?" he said suspiciously. I had some difficulty in convincing him that it was he himself who had been indiscreet.

Bob also played a part in one of PEN's most notable dramas, which was played out in the International Executive Committee at the Dublin Congress.

As I explained earlier, Pierre Emmanuel's first term of office concluded with this Congress, and he had agreed to stand for a further term, but Heinrich Böll had been put up against him. Pierre Emmanuel gracefully expressed his pleasure that Heinrich should be opposing him, and then gave up the chair to Robert Goffin, the distinguished lawyer who was President of the Francophone Belgian Centre and the International Vice-President who had been called upon to stand in for Emmanuel at the Seoul Congress. Goffin was a confirmed bachelor with an explosive temperament and a tendency to hypochondria which meant that he never travelled without a vast armoury of pills. Since in those days there was no procedure laid down for a contested presidential election, it took considerable discussion before it was decided that there should be a secret ballot in which the postal votes of absent Centres should be included. The agreed procedure then was that the head of each delegation should write the name of his Centre's choice on a slip of paper and hand it in to David, who would mark it off on his list of Centres present. This was duly done and Heinrich Böll was declared the winner by 25 votes to 20. What followed I have described earlier. Somehow this contretemps was smoothed over and, after the lunch break, David announced that since certain delegations were dissatisfied with the way in which the election of the International President had been conducted, Bob den Doolaard together with Carlos de Radzitzky (the Belgian baron, jazz-lover and wearer of flamboyant ties, who was Secretary of the Francophone Belgian Centre) – both of them old hands at PEN meetings – would recount the voting papers in the presence of the delegates. This was done, and the final count was 20 votes for Pierre Emmanuel, 24 for Heinrich Böll, and 1 abstention. In this contentious way one of our most distinguished and most delightful International Presidents came to power.

I do not think there was an official post-Congress tour, but Katie and I spent a pleasant day driving in the Wicklow Mountains. On the ferry home we found ourselves in the company of the Israeli delegate, David Shahar, and Vladimir Finkelstein, from the Writers in Exile Centre, who, in a spirit of post-Congress euphoria, serenaded Katie with a song which must have been all too familar to her: "K-k-k-Katie, K-k-k-Katie, you're the only g-g-g-girl that I adore . . ."

10

Dear Kevin,
President Marcos' declaration of martial law has put paid to a Con-
gress in Manila. So instead of being in the Far East again I'm getting
my first impression of West Berlin at a Conference hastily put together
by Thilo Koch, who's a big man in West German television. We've
had a telegram from Kate Nott's sister that Kate won't be with us
because she slipped and fell on the quayside at Harwich. Apparently
she had to endure a very stormy crossing to The Hook and back
before she managed to convince the ferry people that she had broken
her leg. I bet the air was blue! I hope they plied her with plenty of
whisky. Much Love, Elizabeth.

The Conference in West Berlin was held against the backdrop of
the glitter and excitement of that showplace of Western capitalism. I
remember the stunning blue glass in the Kaiser Wilhelm Kirk, the ice
rink, the expensive shops, and an extremely noisy night club called
"The Black Bottom" , to which Thilo took a party of us one evening.
Then there was the Wall. I went on a tour of the Wall with Pavel
Tigrid who, as a Czech exile and a notable Cold War warrior, was
not free to visit East Berlin with the rest of the participants. I recently
found a photograph I had taken of him, unawares, looking over
towards the East with what I interpreted as an exile's longing for
return. Perhaps I was wrong and he was merely thinking how much
better it was in the West. However, all my memories pale before
David's comment when we got home and Gertie asked him how the
meeting had gone. "I think I may say, Gertie, that I was a great
personal success". That saying entered at once into the mythology of
PEN and every time I set off for a Congress thereafter Gertie would
wish me a great personal success!

Heinrich Böll could also have been described as having a great
personal success as International President, although he would never
have dreamed of claiming this for himself. He was a hopeless chairman

of the International Executive Committee because he was so scrupu-
lously fair that, even when some point had been debated ad nauseam
and the rest of us were waiting anxiously for him to move on to the
next item on the agenda, he would still be looking round to see if
there was anyone else who wanted to speak. This was an insignificant
defect, however, in a man of such shining integrity and disarming
modesty that we all loved him.

The first meeting of the International Executive Committee which
he had to chair took place at the English-Speaking Union in London
in April 1972. There was the usual heated discussion concerning censorship in Eastern Europe, in which the formidable President of Bulgarian PEN, Leda Mileva, played a leading role. It was noticeable,
however, that the second Bulgarian delegate, Nikolai Antonov, took
no part in this discussion. This was probably because Leda carried
sufficient fire-power on her own, and did not need his support. It
might also have had something to do with his love-lorn condition. In
the true spirit of PEN, he had not allowed political barriers to stand
in his way, but had developed a passion for Nancy Ing, who was
there to represent the Chinese Centre in Taipei. Nancy was deeply
embarrassed by his pursuit and gave him no encouragement, so he
was reduced to casting smouldering looks in her direction, which must
have taken his mind off the business in hand!

It was probably when Heinrich came to London for this meeting
that there was a dinner for the delegates at the Criterion. Gertie, who
had been interrupted in the process of dying her hair the evening
before and was trying therefore to be as inconspicuous as possible to
conceal her parti-coloured coiffure, found him lurking shyly behind
a pillar in the entrance hall. "Aren't you coming up to the restaurant
Herr Böll?" she said to him in German. "Yes, if you'll come with
me", he replied trustingly. So, they made a grand entrance together.

*

To KEVIN FITZGERALD   *Rönneberga, Sweden*
Crossways, Chinnor, Oxon   *May, 1973*

Dear Kevin,
We're conferring at a trade union centre on a lake outside Stockholm.
It feels as if we're miles from anywhere – nothing to distract us from
the serious business of our discussions! The accommodation is fairly
basic: bedroom huts separate from the central reception area and
restaurant. Carlos de Radzitzky, our Belgian baron, is furious that he

can't have breakfast in his room – something that he says has never happened to him before in his entire life! Much love, Elizabeth

---

The Rönneberga Conference was organised by Per Wästberg and, because of his lifelong interest in African literature, Wole Soyinka and other black writers were there, which made a refreshing change. Because the conference centre was rather cut off, so delegates could not sneak out of meetings and go shopping or sight-seeing, the bus trip into Stockholm to hear Heinrich Böll deliver his Nobel Prize Lecture was particularly welcome. We sat on three sides of a square whilst Heinrich delivered his speech, which was lengthy and in German, and I was so placed that I could watch David and Peter in profile and, knowing that neither of them understood a word of German, was impressed by their expressions of earnest attention. The only give-away was that Peter put on his glasses, which I recognised to be a cover-up in case he fell asleep!

After the speech we all adjourned for a good party. The sequel to this was that, on his return to Rönneberga, Per, mildly inebriated, went, as he thought, to his suite and opened it with his organiser's master key. The first thing he saw on the table in the sitting room was a bowl of nuts and a pile of the poetry of Z. Rahnema, the Iranian delegate. This did not strike him as strange because Dr. Rahnema, on his arrival, had presented Per with some volumes of his poetry and some nuts, thinking, no doubt, that this would smooth his path to the Nobel Prize. Per therefore started to get undressed, but had only got to the stage of taking his shirt off when he heard a rustle from the bedroom. This surprised him because his partner, Margareta Ekström, had stayed in Stockholm and was to come on later. Saying: "Is that you, darling?", he went into the bedroom, only to find Madame Rahnema sitting up in bed. They both screamed and he ran out, clutching his shirt, to find his way to his proper suite, which was in the same position but on a different floor. History does not relate where Dr. Rahnema was when his wife's honour was apparently being threatened!

On the last night at Rönneberga Carlos de Radzitzky and David, friends and fellow *bon viveurs* for many years, sat up late into the night drinking together. Since David's room was next to mine and the dividing walls were thin, I was disturbed and rather annoyed by this, particularly since I was then awakened early by the melancholy noise of the seagulls from the lake. When David became ill the following year and we all realised that there would be no more international meetings for him, I forgot my resentment and was glad that his last meeting had finished in such a characteristic fashion.

*

It was during the summer of 1973 that David first complained that his hands were losing their grip; he could no longer pick up the soap in the bath and he found it difficult to grasp the steering wheel of his car. Since he was a great hypochondriac, inclined to visit a specialist if he had a pain in his big toe, none of us in the office took his complaints very seriously. We even laughed when the specialist he did visit told him that he had motor neurone disease (which very few had heard of in those days) and he consulted his medical dictionary and told us that it was incurable. "Trust David to have an incurable disease", Liz said. When winter came he complained of trouble with his back and almost stopped coming in to the office. Since Liz had moved into the Carver household, where both Blanche and David required nursing care, this left me to organise the English Centre meetings as well as handling the day-to-day business of International PEN. I remember saying rather acidly to V. S. Pritchett (who had by then succeeded L. P. Hartley as President of English PEN) that I thought it was really the winter weather which David did not like. "You mean he'll come up like a crocus in the spring?" VSP said, conjuring up a pleasing vision of a large purple crocus. This was the last time I laughed about David's condition.

After Blanche's stroke, all the Carvers' friends had expected her to die before David and, since most of the money they lived on came from her first husband's estate and would go, on her death, to her son Jeremy, we had worried about how David would adapt to a reduced lifestyle. It turned out otherwise. He became steadily more disabled and finally had to be taken into the Hospital for Nervous Diseases in Queen Square where, early in May 1974, the effects of the disease reached his diaphragm and stopped his breathing, so that, mercifully, he did not linger on, aware but totally paralysed, as he might have done. His last days were very sad, because he was so much afraid of death that he feared to let himself go to sleep at night in case he did not wake up in the morning. After his death Blanche was moved to a nursing home in the country and only survived him by a few months.

Part II

PETER ELSTOB

The King is Dead. Long Live The King

1

Throughout this time Peter had not only been a great support to David, but also to us at the office. Several weeks before David's death David had appointed Peter as his deputy, and so, as International Press Officer and David's closest colleague, Peter found himself catapulted reluctantly into the position of Acting International Secretary, and prepared to attend in that capacity the International Conference which was to take place on May 19 and 20 in Ohrid (Macedonia). Not long before he and I and Katie were due to leave for Ohrid, he rang me and said, with forced calm, that his wife Barbara had had a stroke and was still unconscious, so he might not be able to get to the meeting. Feeling stunned by this accumulation of disasters, I said weakly, after sympathising with him: "But who will handle the election of the International President if you're not there?" "You will, of course, my dear," he replied bracingly. It was clearly not the moment to express my doubts about my competence to undertake this task, so I swallowed and said: "Of course."

As it turned out, I did not have to handle the presidential election. Barbara Elstob recovered consciousness and courageously insisted that Peter should go to Ohrid, and he caught, with the skin of his teeth, the plane which the English delegates were travelling on – being driven on to the tarmac just before the plane took off.

Katie and I had an even more dramatic journey. On the day we had to travel in order to arrive at Ohrid two days in advance of the Conference, there was no direct flight to Skopje. We therefore had to change planes in Belgrade. This we did in a big thunderstorm, which, since there were no facilities at Skopje airport for pilots to be talked down in poor visibility, prevented our plane landing there. Twice we took off from Belgrade and circled the airport at Skopje, and twice we returned to Belgrade without having succeeded in landing. By the time of our second return it was late in the evening, all the facilities at Belgrade airport had closed down, and everyone who spoke English among the airport staff had gone home. It was clear that we were going to have to spend the night there (there was some big conference in Belgrade, so no hotel rooms were available in the city), but we were very disconcerted when an official came round and, without explanation, tore up our plane tickets. How were we going to get to Skopje? We naively assumed that a bus was bound to be laid on in the morning, but a lawyer from Washington who was also stranded at the airport and seemed to be the only other English-speaking person there, depressed us by saying that there was no obligation in Yugoslavia to make sure that passengers reached their destination. There might well not be a bus. Visions of hitchhiking with a portable typewriter and all the PEN documents were not encouraging. Nonetheless, we were tired so we spread ourselves out on two benches and went to sleep. I was awakened a short time later by a policeman shaking me by the shoulder and pointing angrily to my feet. He clearly felt that they were sullying the purity of the leatherette cover of the bench. Seeing the gun at his belt, I did not feel inclined to argue, so I sat up and spent the rest of the night watching parties of businessmen – evidently used to the vagaries of travel in Yugoslavia – cheerfully whiling away the time by weighing each other on the luggage scales.

In the early hours some ham sandwiches suddenly turned up. Even more miraculously, a bus did appear in the morning, and we and our luggage were packed aboard it. We drove all day and arrived in Skopje just in time to catch the last car from the Macedonian PEN office bound for Ohrid. We were squashed into the back with the typewriters and, since the mountain road was winding, I started to feel rather queasy. We stopped at the top of the pass and I was offered a bowl of yoghourt, but I did not fancy it. However, I started feeling better when we had wound down the other side and saw the hotel, which was beautifully situated right on the shore of Lake Ohrid, looking across to Albania.

*

---

to KEVIN FITZGERALD   *Ohrid, Macedonia*
Crossways, Chinnor, Oxon   *May 1974*

Dear Kevin,
You will have heard the sad news of David's death and that Peter has, temporarily at least, stepped into his shoes. The King is dead, Long Live the King! We're here at a Conference in Yugoslav Macedonia after a very adventurous journey which I'll tell you about when you next give me lunch at The Athenaeum. Lake Ohrid is set among beautiful mountains. We're promised an excursion to see some of the wonderful frescoes in the churches round about. Much love,
Elizabeth

The hotel restaurant boasted a very impressive menu, but we soon discovered that it was largely fictional and it was better to ignore it and find out what was really on offer. One morning, just as we were finishing breakfast, Peter said to me idly: "I wonder what 'ham and eggs' is in Macedonian". He repeated the question to Bob den Doolaard (an expert on Yugoslavia), who happened to be passing, and Bob, reacting like the man of action that he was, started spinning round, clicking his fingers and summoning waiters from every direction and demanding what sounded like "amandix". It took some time to explain that Peter had finished breakfast and did not actually want ham and eggs on the spot.

At the meeting of the International Executive Committee Peter was confirmed as Acting International Secretary until the Congress which was to take place in Jerusalem in December. V. S. Pritchett was elected to succeed Heinrich Böll as International President. Per Wästberg was also a candidate, but conceded defeat gracefully when the vote went 29 to 15 against him. The most prominent delegate was Talat Halman, who had been present at the Dun Laoghaire Congress in 1971 as Turkish Minister of Culture and had invited us all to a Congress in Istanbul the following year. The change of regime in Turkey had aborted this plan and caused Talat to take up a lecturing post at Princeton University, so he now appeared as a delegate for the American Centre. His skill as a linguist was very much in evidence when he upstaged VSP at the end of the meeting by thanking our hosts in Serbo-Croat – probably in Macedonian as well! He also rivalled Leda Mileva as an expert on procedure.

In the course of the conference there was a banquet at which the guest of honour was a Vice-President of Yugoslavia. Security was tight, with an armed guard on every door. Somehow, through this cordon, word reached Peter that his daughter Sukey was trying to get him on the phone. He forced his way out, with some difficulty, thinking that there might be bad news about Barbara. When he had re-entered the room, with equal difficulty, he said to Per, who was sitting next to him: "Thank God, it was only a message from the police to say that my car has been blown up"! This sounded like the final blow in the catalogue of disasters, but was a false alarm. An I.R.A. bomb had exploded in the long-term car park at Heathrow, but it turned out that Peter's car was not, after all, one of the ones that had been destroyed.

At the same banquet, the Egyptian delegate, Mursi Saad El-Din, a practised flirt, was making a play for Lavinia Derwent, who was equally practised at dealing with such advances. During an unscheduled pause in one of the speeches the respectful hush was interrupted by an unintentionally audible riposte from Lavinia: "We'll just wait till the wee man has finished speaking, then we'll have it off under the table".

The Scottish delegation, with their customary habit of adopting waifs and strays, had taken under their wing a Turkish poet, who had mysteriously appeared at the conference, with no money and nowhere to sleep. Owing to the language barrier, they could not decide whether it was Cliff or Lavinia that the poet fancied, but Cliff generously allowed him to sleep on the spare bed in his room. At breakfast on the first morning I asked Cliff how the night had gone. "He only took his socks off", Cliff reported, "Och but he *snorred*".

2

Back in London we organised a Memorial Evening for David at the English-Speaking Union. It was well-attended and very moving. We played a tape of David singing his favourite party piece: "The Bonnie Earl of Murray", and various people made speeches honouring his memory. Robert Goffin gave a dramatic rendering of "In Flanders fields the poppies blow", with particular emotional emphasis on the passage:

> "If you break faith with us who die
> We shall not sleep, though poppies grow
> In Flanders fields".

The whole evening was rather overshadowed for me by the arrangement proposed by Theodora Olembert, a long-standing member of English PEN, that a select few of those present be invited to go on to a buffet supper at her wealthy cousin's flat in Belgravia. Theodora herself, a Polish immigrant film-maker, was practically penniless, but her cousin was married to a Greek banker and would be delighted (according to Theodora) to entertain twenty or thirty of the foreign visitors. When I said that surely her cousin would like to know the exact number so as to be sure of having enough plates and forks, Theodora replied airily that if there were more people than expected her cousin could send her chauffeur to her other house to fetch more plates and forks. My doubts turned out to be fully justified as, when I arrived a little late at the house after attempting, not entirely successfully, to separate those who had been invited from those who had not, I found the reception rooms of the rather small flat packed with PEN members more inclined to grumble because the strawberries had run out than to admire the Rembrandts on the walls.

Peter meanwhile, had had to grapple with David's legacy to PEN of an overdraft of £10,000, which the Midland Bank had inadvertently allowed to accumulate without any security. He was assisted in this by John Paxton, who had taken on the job of Joint Treasurer of English PEN while David was still alive, and was persuaded by Peter to stay on when David died. John had been Editor of *The Statesman's Yearbook* for many years, as well as editing many other reference books, and the impression he gave of being "a safe pair of hands" was entirely merited. He introduced the item "State of Play" to the agendas of the English PEN Finance Committee, which lent a soothing aura of cricket on the village green to the chaotic state of PEN's finances. In addition Peter got Thilo Koch, who, as Secretary of West German PEN, had organised the very successful Berlin Conference in 1972, to agree to stand for election as International Treasurer. This was a stroke of genius because it succeeded both in giving a more international aspect to the International Secretariat and enabling us to pay off the overdraft by virtue of a grant which Thilo managed to obtain from the Krupp Foundation. Thilo's work as a television journalist kept him busy, so he seldom had time to spare to come to London. The keeping of the accounts was left to Bill Barazetti, who, by good fortune, was also a native German speaker, having been born in German Switzerland. Bill had come to us in late 1973, taking on from his daughter Kathy the challenging task of balancing the PEN accounts. In addition to the knowledge of international affairs which he had gained as General Secretary for many years of the Public Services' International Union, he had a talent , which continued to serve PEN well for many years, for keeping his counsel and then producing money as if by magic when required.

The other measure which Peter and John took was to close the Glebe House bar and restaurant, which, in spite of Linda's efforts, had been losing money disastrously. This meant that, in the new regime of strict economy, there was no longer a job for Liz Warner. Katie Ryde had left of her own accord, so, on the secretarial side, there was just me (now, thanks to Peter, transmogrified into "Administrative Secretary"). We decided that I could manage with a part-time secretarial assistant, and so engaged Barbara Towle, a large and handsome lady with a jolly laugh who had served in the Wrens and now lived just round the corner in Chelsea Manor Street. She initiated various reforms of office procedure, the most important of which was to get an addressograph firm to take on the membership mailings (which had in the past been done by teams of volunteers – usually Lizzie's boy friends – stuffing the envelopes and taking them round to the sorting office in relays). She also reorganised the filing and taught me the valuable fact that paperclips are death to any filing system.

3

To KEVIN FITZGERALD   *Jerusalem*
Crossways, Chinnor, Oxon   *December 1974*

Dear Kevin,
After a postponement because of the Yom Kippur War we've reached
the Holy City at last. Josephine Pullein-Thompson is representing
English PEN instead of the late lamented Paul. Like Mary T. she
writes pony books but seems a more down-to-earth character. Michael
Rubinstein is busy squiring that indomitable old lady Amabel Clough-
Ellis round all the sights. Our hosts seem likely to run us into the
ground in their determination that we should see everything. Love
Elizabeth

The official delegates chosen to represent English PEN at the Congress
in Jerusalem in December 1974 were Michael Rubinstein, PEN's
honorary solicitor, and Paul Tabori, the Hungarian exile who had
been active in PEN for many years, creator of the Writers in Prison
Committee, tireless worker and originator of countless award schemes
and publishing projects, and close friend of David's. Sadly, Paul died
of a heart attack in the same year as David and not long before the
Congress. The well-known children's writer, Josephine Pullein-
Thompson, a recent recruit to the English PEN Executive Committee,
was chosen to take his place, thus setting her feet on the path to the
eventual presidency of the English Centre. More importantly to me,
it was the beginning of a very rewarding friendship.

All the delegates were quartered at the Diplomat Hotel and, since
the Israeli PEN were assiduous in making sure that we saw as much
of their country as possible, the business of the Congress was inter-
spersed with two optional all-day tours, when we were on the go from
early in the morning until late in the evening, without much time to
stop for refreshment. Josephine and I and Sukey Elstob (then a teen-
ager, who had come with Peter and Barbara to the Congress) all took
advantage of the opportunities offered and, exhausted, forgathered
afterwards in the hotel coffee bar to revive ourselves. That was when
Sukey and I got hooked on Josephine's tales of the rival covens she

had discovered on the Isle of Man when she was doing research into witchcraft for one of her books, and of respectable middle class citizens being discovered by the fire brigade dancing naked round a bonfire on Beltane's Night.

The all-day tours, one to Galilee and the other to Masada and the Dead Sea, were spectacular, but also very long. The tour of Galilee included a visit to a kibbutz, where we arrived too late for lunch and were treated to many speeches, each translated consecutively from Hebrew or Arabic into English and French. On the top of Masada we were able to quash our guide's suggestion that one of our number should read aloud the apocryphal speech of the captain of the defenders invented by Josephus. The towering cliffs were sufficiently impressive without that, and in addition we were all shivering in the cold wind on the top. On the way back from Masada we paused by the Dead Sea and were invited to take a dip. Only the English crime novelist Celia Fremlin (fully clad) and a very tall and skinny Danish poet called Jorgen Sønne (stripped to his underpants) took up this invitation. The rest of us paddled, and found ourselves quite uncomfortably sticky enough as it was for the bus ride back to Jerusalem.

At the beginning of the week we had been taken to Yad Vashem, where, after we had been shown the piles of children's shoes, the photographs and other horrifying exhibits, there was a moving moment when Heinrich Böll, standing by the sacred flame, bowed his head and said, with great emotion: "I have read about this; I have written about this; but I cannot speak about this". He and V.S.P. then, wearing yarmulkes, lit candles from the flame and stood in silent remembrance.

On the Thursday evening there was a reception given by the President of Israel, Professor Ephraim Katzir, at his residence. This was another occasion when there was some trouble about protocol. Our hosts had intended that our International President, VSP, should have a private audience with President Katzir. Dorothy Pritchett soon scotched any idea that she should be left out of this, so the Pritchetts were taken off to another room. Robert Goffin felt that he, as the only International Vice-President at the Congress, should have been included and, in his anger at Peter, whom he blamed for this omission, took him by the lapels of his jacket and shook him. Fortunately Peter accepted this treatment with his usual good grace and managed to calm the old man down.

Peter had come to Jerusalem still as Acting International Secretary. A Selection Committee had met since Ohrid and put forward his name and that of Jean de Beer, Secretary of French PEN, as rival candidates for the permanent post. Peter had always sworn that nothing would induce him to take on David's job, but the prospect of International Headquarters being captured by the French and taken to Paris was enough to change his mind. He was, however, astonished to receive from Pierre Emmanuel, as President of French PEN, a telegram announcing that Jean de Beer's accreditation as French delegate had been withdrawn. When he showed this to Jean de Beer, Jean went white and asked what Peter intended to do about it. He must have been surprised when Peter replied that he had already cabled Pierre Emmanuel to tell him that, even though he was President of French PEN, he had no authority to withdraw Jean's accreditation without consulting his Executive Committee. In any case the election for International Secretary proceeded and Peter carried the day by 28 votes to 10. Jean de Beer, swallowing his disappointment, said that he was very happy with the result and at the fact that for the first time in its history PEN had a democratically elected International Secretary. This was a posthumous dig at David, with whom Jean had always had a love-hate relationship, where an embrace might be the prelude to a metaphorical knife in the back.

The Jerusalem Congress finished just before Christmas and, instead of going home for the usual Paterson family gathering, I went south with the Elstobs to spend six days baking in the sun at Eilat, on the top of the Gulf of Aqbar. According to the tourist posters this has since been developed as a popular resort, but in 1974 the money to build it had run out as a consequence of the 1967 war and I remember it as largely consisting of half-built concrete hotels and apartment blocks. We were not the only refugees from the Congress. On our arrival we found a message waiting for us at the desk telling us that the best Polish vodka was on offer in Hut Number Six. (Our hotel was arranged like a motel, with bedroom huts grouped round a central reception block.) This turned out to come from Pavel and Ivana Tigrid, who had caught an earlier plane. We were also joined by Marion Hunter, a member of English PEN who, having rebelled against her Aberdonian father's view that the only training a woman needed was in domestic science, had established herself as a translator from French and Italian. The French she had learnt at school, but the Italian she had picked up whilst living in a derelict palazzo in Venice. Attracted by her sympathetic expression and soft Scottish voice, complete strangers sitting next to her on aeroplanes would tell her their life stories, which she always listened to with friendly interest. I found her very entertaining company, although not sharing her unquestioning belief in astrology, on which she was something of an expert.

We followed our own devices during the day, but often met at Raffy's Bar on the beach in the evenings. Peter had hired a car and I went with him, Barbara and Sukey on various excursions into the desert. On one of these we followed a road which led to a laboratory built into the hillside. In spite of the fact that the entrance was plastered with red notices saying what was obviously the Hebrew equivalent of "Top Secret – Keep Out", Peter parked the car and, disregarding the protests of his passengers, vanished inside. To our great relief he emerged shortly afterwards, having found the place deserted. We guessed that this was Israel's nuclear research station, but if so the scientists were evidently all at lunch and no guards had been posted.

On another, less alarming, excursion, we swam in the warm water of the Red Sea and picnicked on a beach from which we could look across to Saudi Arabia.

When our six days were up the Elstobs and the Tigrids flew back to Tel Aviv to connect with their flights home, but Marion and I decided to travel by bus up the length of Israel so as to get more idea of the countryside. It was a long, hot journey and unfortunately the bus had its usual soporific effect on me so that I slept most of the way. Occasionally I would wake up and Marion would say: "We passed a very interesting herd of camels a little way back." "Why on earth didn't you wake me?" I asked indignantly, but it was too late.

*

I next saw Amabel Williams-Ellis (widow of the architect Clough Williams-Ellis) at a joint meeting which English PEN and the Progressive League held at the Conference Centre at Hoddesdon the following year. Although she had been a member of PEN for a long time I had never seen her at any of our meetings until she turned up at the Jerusalem Congress. That had evidently given her a taste for more and she was the first person I saw when I went into the Conference Centre lounge to find some tea. She greeted me like a white explorer stranded amongst savages who sees the relief party approaching.

"Bring your tea over here, my dear" she said, and then, glancing round at the assembled members of the Progressive League and not attempting to modulate her carrying tones: "What very odd looking people these are". I was rather inclined to agree with her, but changed the subject hastily.

The Progressive League was founded at roughly the same time as PEN, in the twenties, for people who believed in free sex, country dancing and the open air and liked to satisfy these urges by meeting at weekend conferences. I think the original members tended to wear beards and sandals when neither of those things were fashionable. Many of them were would-be writers, and so Celia Fremlin, a League member who was also a successful published writer, had a great following amongst them. As she was also a member of the English PEN Committee, it was she who had arranged that PEN should provide the speakers for the Hoddesdon weekend.

Most of us in the PEN contingent were, like Amabel Williams-Ellis, rather dubious about the company we found ourselves in. As soon as we arrived we trooped down into the town to visit the off licence and came back fortified with liquor to drink at bedroom parties if the going got too tough. In fact it was quite a pleasant weekend, with walks in the autumn countryside and a good evening's discussion about crime writing. We none of us participated in the country danc-ing, but peered sheepishly through the windows from outside to watch the Progressive League performing.

Considering the rather high age level of the membership, the League seemed to be remarkably active, not only at country dancing, but in putting their belief in free love into practice. One of the PEN members (I think it was Francis King) found his bed invaded in the middle of the night by a small bearded man who, when they had both recovered from their surprise, explained that he had thought he was joining his lady friend who was normally allocated that room.

I was put to sleep in a partitioned off cubicle in a long line of such cubicles which reminded me of the dormitories at my boarding school. There was no sound-proofing so I was very embarrassed when, having gone to bed early on the Saturday evening, I found that my immediate neighbour had also left the dance floor, but in her case not to sleep but to make love. Since I'd turned my light off they could have had no idea that I was trapped there as an unwilling auditor of the lovers' proceedings. Inevitably I recognised their voices, and so knew that it was because the man's wife was also present that weekend that they were having to carry on in this clandestine way.

A happier event was the coming together of a very drink-sodden John Braine and that kind and sensible woman, Janet Barber, who became his mistress and gave him a great deal of happiness for the rest of his life.

4

To KEVIN FITZGERALD   *Vienna*
Crossways, Chinnor, Oxon   *November 1975*

Dear Kevin,
We've been given the privilege of launching the Vienna Hilton on the
world, so are accommodated in great state. It promises to be a splendid
Congress altogether. Included in the programme, as well as a visit to
the Spanish Riding Stables, is a night at the Opera. I'm not sure
whether my wardrobe can stand the strain! Much love, Elizabeth

Unfortunately the presidential suite allotted to Victor and Dorothy
Pritchett in the Vienna Hilton had the disadvantage of being next
door to that of Eugene Ionescu and his wife, who kept the Pritchetts
awake by their noisy and prolonged quarrels. The secretarial suite,
on the other hand, which Peter and I shared, was very comfortable
and quiet: a large sitting-room separating our two bedrooms. This
was very convenient for the series of International Secretary's drinks
parties, a custom which Peter had initiated in those days when there
were seldom more than a hundred official delegates at a Congress. It
was a headache to make sure that no delegates were left out and that
enemies were kept apart, but it did help to accentuate the friendly
atmosphere of PEN, enabling delegates to speak and associate more
freely than they felt able to in the Committee meetings.

The Vienna meeting of the International Executive Committee was
a particularly acrimonious one, a cockpit for the contestants in PEN's
own Cold War, and Victor needed all Peter's support to keep order
from the chair. It is strange how the issues which then seemed likely
to dog us for the rest of the century, if not beyond, are now so much
a part of history.

The East German delegation threatened a walk-out in protest at the
donation which Thilo Koch had obtained from the Krupp Foundation,
which they considered to be tainted money because Alfred Krupp had
made his fortune by the manufacture of arms. Victor Pritchett pointed
out that many worthy Foundations, such as the Carnegie, had been
established as an act of restitution by men who had made their money

in questionable ways. Twinkling benevolently behind his glasses, he expressed his distress at the GDR Centre's reaction and asked what could be done. "Should we give the money back?" he asked innocently, adding that this might be seen as PEN trying to relive two world wars for its own moral sustenance. Since the East Germans knew perfectly well that to return the money would leave PEN bankrupt, they had reluctantly to pipe down.

The International Press Officer whose job it was to produce suitably edited reports of the Committee meetings for the press was John Peet, newly appointed to that job by Peter. His appointment had raised some eyebrows, notably in the English Centre, some of whose members regarded him as a traitor. John, who sported a moustache like a caricature of a "wizard prang" Second World War RAF officer, was a convinced communist. The last report he had filed as Reuters' correspondent in West Berlin, had been of his own defection to East Berlin. Since then he had edited the English language newspaper there, *The Democratic Report*. As Peter explained to those who objected that John might give a communist bias to his reporting, John was an experienced professional journalist and far too intelligent to do anything so obvious. Whatever his political views, he was a very likeable and amusing man and his appointment effectively muzzled the complaints which the delegates from Eastern Europe were always inclined to make about the reporting of PEN meetings.

In accordance with the usual practice in those days of delegates to PEN Congresses being received by the Head of State of the host country, in Vienna in 1975 we were all invited to meet the Chancellor, Bruno Kreisky. Waiting in the corridor of the Chancellory, the Pritchetts, Peter and I found ourselves standing outside the door of the room where the Congress of Vienna had been held in 1815. It was a heavy and impressive door, with a large and impressive key, which Dorothy dared Peter to pocket. Back in London some time later she asked Peter what he had done with the key. When he protested his innocence, she said: "Oh yes, I remember. It seemed so uncharacteristic of you".

A sad postcript to the Vienna Congress was the death soon afterwards of the Secretary of the Austrian Centre, Reinhard Federmann, who had organised the meeting with self-effacing efficiency despite suffering from cancer.

5

To KEVIN FITZGERALD   *Taipei*
Crossways, Chinnor, Oxon   *April 1976*

Dear Kevin,
Peter and Barbara Elstob and I are attending a Conference here. Our
chief official duty has been to visit the tomb of Chiang Kai-shek, who
has died since our 1970 visit. Peter and I did this, bowing low three
times as instructed by our guides. Otherwise we're being well looked
after by our friend Nancy Ing and gorging ourselves on delicious
Chinese food. Much love, Elizabeth.

1976 was a year into which we somehow managed to cram three
international meetings. In April Barbara Elstob and I set off for Hong
Kong (Barbara still somewhat disabled after her stroke, so that we
were given the V.I.P. wheel chair treatment) to meet Peter, who had
gone ahead of us via Bangkok and Korea. After a night in Hong Kong,
which I found had lost the magic it had had for me in 1970 and
seemed tawdry and noisy, we all went on to Taiwan to attend the
Fourth Asian Writers' Conference. The theme of this, I see from the
printed proceedings, was *Thirty Years of Turmoil in Asian Literature*,
but nothing of the discussion has stayed in my mind. I remember the
splendours of the Mandarin Hotel, an ornate red and gold structure
like a giant pavilion, built by Nancy's husband Glyn, and delightful
social occasions such as the Mongolian Barbecue. This took place in
the open air, and, after we had eaten, everyone was expected to perform a party piece. Some of our hosts showed an unsuspected talent
for singing arias from Chinese Opera (an acquired taste, I found!). I
shrank into the background, and it was left to Peter to redeem the
honour of the International Secretariat by a vigorous rendering of
"There is a tavern in the town". The Tigrids were also there, and
Nancy, with that imaginative generosity which I was to come to know
so well, took Barbara, Ivana Tigrid and me to her tailor to be
measured. Splendid cheongsams for all of us were produced in an
incredibly short time, and at each subsequent international meeting
Nancy brought me another one, until the Stockholm Congress in 1978,

when, trying to change for dinner in a hurry, I got stuck halfway into Nancy's latest gift and, since cheongsams are tubular, could neither get in nor out. I had to phone for help to Peter, who was in his suite waiting for Nancy and John Paxton to join us for dinner and who rushed along the corridor to my room in a great hurry, pulled the dress off me, and rushed back to his room so as not to keep his guests waiting, thereby no doubt arousing wild conjectures in the mind of a fellow-guest who happened to be passing at the time and must have caught a glimpse of my half-naked form as Peter hurried out. I had to break it as tactfully as possible to Nancy that her tailor had unfortunately confused my measurements with Ivana Tigrid's much more elegant proportions.

*

To KEVIN FITZGERALD   *The Hague*
Crossways, Chinnor, Oxon   *May 1976*

Dear Kevin,
We were scarcely back from the Far East when we were off to Holland
– my first visit. We're, staying at the Hotel des Indes, not as flashy as
the Vienna Hilton or the Mandarin in Taipei, but a former palace
nonetheless so just about up to our standard. Displayed in its lobby
are signatures of all the famous people such as Eisenhower and Chur-
chill who have stayed here. It's in a very pleasant, quiet backwater
of the city. Much love, Elizabeth

The Hague Conference was a lively and informal meeting, presided over by Theun de Vries, whose election as President of Dutch PEN had caused some controversy in that Centre because it was only in 1968, after the Russian tanks had rolled into Prague, that he had renounced his long-standing allegiance to the communist party. It was a tribute to both men that he and Bob den Doolaard (a vigorous opponent of communism, as of any form of totalitarianism) always remained friends.

As well as enjoying cuisine from the Dutch East Indies and visits to the homes of members of Dutch PEN, we had time to go to Amsterdam and take a boat trip on the canals. My souvenir of the occasion is an ashtray which Pavel gave me which bears the legend: "This ashtray was stolen from the Amstel Hotel"!

The International Executive Committee was firmly chaired by Per, in the absence of VSP. Under the item "Future Conferences", the German Branch of the Writers in Exile Centre repeated the invitation, which had been accepted in Vienna, for an International PEN Conference to be held in Hamburg in May 1977. There was uneasiness about this invitation, especially amongst the East European Centres, on the grounds that, since all the members of the Writers in Exile Centre appeared to be exiles from socialist countries, the meeting was likely to be used for purposes of anti-communist propaganda and therefore no delegates from Eastern Europe would attend it. Pavel Tigrid made the rather surprising statement that his Centre had never, in public or private, in writing or by the spoken word, attacked a socialist regime. He also affirmed that it was untrue to say that all their members were exiles from socialist countries. He concluded the discussion on a defiant note, saying that his Centre's invitation to Hamburg still stood and preparations for the meeting would go ahead.

*

Pavel was proved to be right, but before Hamburg came the London Congress, which was organised on a shoe-string and held in August 1976 in one of the hottest English summers on record. It was Peter's idea that the best way to restore PEN's fortunes and raise its public profile would be to hold a Congress in London, twenty years after the last one, which had been held in 1956 with John Lehmann as Chairman of the Organising Committee. Many of the English PEN Executive were aghast at the idea, exclaiming that the country was at the bottom of a depression and it would be impossible to raise the necessary funds. But Peter persisted, and Stephen Spender, as a literary figure well-known abroad as well as at home, was persuaded to become President of English PEN for that year. One of the preliminary meetings to discuss the organisation of the Congress was held in John Lehmann's flat. Relations between him and Stephen were notoriously brittle, and were not helped when Stephen accidentally knocked an obviously valuable vase off a side table. John Lehmann went white, but, gritting his teeth as he looked at the shattered remains, said: "It's quite all right. It doesn't matter at all". In spite of this inauspicious start, a small Organising Committee was set up and, at its first meeting, each member was given some task to perform. Josephine, probably because of her wide experience of organizing Pony Club events, was asked to get estimates for delegates' badges. At the second meeting of the committee she was the only person to have performed her appointed task, and she had done it with her usual thoroughness. This helped to convince Peter that she was the right person to be appointed Chair of the Committee. Once she took on the organisation the success of the Congress was assured, even if, like L. P. Hartley, she found foreign names a problem and therefore privately rechristened many of the delegates, so that Iván Boldizsár, became "Dr. Balderdash", and a prominent member of the Writers in Exile Centre called István Csicery-Ronay, became "Mr. Chicory".

In spite of Lord Butler agreeing to sign umpteen appeal letters to firms and companies, practically no money was raised, so the Congress had to take place at the Penta (now the Forum), a very functional package holiday hotel on the Cromwell Road, where the bedrooms were each equipped with a kettle and a small oven so that guests could make their own breakfast coffee and heat their own croissants from the supplies left outside their rooms on trays the night before. The West German delegation complained that their trays were constantly being stolen; some other delegations unkindly suggested that this was a put-up job so that the Germans could eat a much more ample breakfast in the Coffee Shop. I was posted at the Penta to deal with problems that might occur during the night, when everyone else on the Organizing Committee had gone home. My usefulness in this role can be judged by the fact that on the one night that the smoke alarm went off and all the delegates gathered in deshabille in the hotel lobby in the early hours, I was woken by an odd noise and, not being able to track down its source, went back to sleep again.

By some clever arrangement Peter managed to make the Congress self-financing, having got such a good price for a block booking made well in advance that the amount unofficial delegates paid for their rooms covered the accommodation costs of the official delegates, for which the host Centre was responsible. The British Government would not contribute any money to the Congress, but they did give a reception in the splendid setting of the Banqueting Hall in Whitehall, which was attended by Lord Donaldson, as Minister for the Arts. As usual on such occasions, his speech was embarrassingly almost entirely drowned by the noise of delegates talking and eating.

Other parties during the Congress were given at The Guildhall, The British Library and County Hall, and, since none of these venues could accommodate the entire 700 or so Congress participants, the events were held simultaneously. This gave us the delicate task of dividing the participants up in such a way that there did not seem to be a "top" or a "bottom" party. In spite of this, everyone assumed that The Guildhall was the most desirable party to be at, and County Hall the least. In this they were mistaken; those of us who went to County Hall had the best time because we had our drinks on the terrace by the river, looking over towards the Houses of Parliament, the perfect way to pass a hot summer evening.

Peter had decreed that an essential expense was to hire official limousines to take the V.I.P.'s between the Penta and the various other Congress venues, and one of my main concerns came to be connecting Stephen with his limousine. He was a most obliging and obedient President, but somehow he and his limousine always seemed to be in different places, so that I am not sure whether he ever actually succeeded in riding in it. I do remember that I for some reason dispatched him to the South Bank at the wrong moment, and got an agitated telephone call from the Festival Hall to say that a tall, red-faced, white-haired man, who said he was the President of PEN, was standing in the lobby and seemed to be lost.

The Opening Ceremony was held in the Queen Elizabeth Hall, with Arthur Koestler giving the keynote speech on the Keatsian theme of "The Truth of the Imagination". In spite of the non-political nature of the subject, Heinz Kamnitzer, on behalf of the GDR Centre, made a statement in the International Executive Committee objecting to the choice of Koestler because of his known anti-communism. Victor Pritchett, from the Chair, after paying a disarming tribute to Professor Kamnitzer's good humour and intelligence, explained that English PEN had chosen as principal speakers for the Congress writers like Koestler who would attract an audience because they were well-known on the Continent as well as in England. This was also intended to counter the criticism sometimes aimed at English writers, particularly those of VSP's own generation, that they lived very comfortably within their own political system, entirely cut off from the Continent and not understanding the Continental mind. Since Koestler had arrived in England from troubled times abroad long ago he had slowly evolved and perhaps become almost as sleepy as the English writers themselves. He was now apologetic about the political stage of his development and even took an interest in Keats, which VSP himself thought was rather a good idea, but many people more actively engaged in politics might wonder about. The only thing in the GDR statement which really roused VSP's ire was its reference to Koestler's "all-round image". He said that if there was one word more than another to which he objected in the English language at the present moment, it was the word "image". He liked reality, not these projections which were put across by the press. Perhaps he himself had an "image", but he was ignorant of it and would deeply resent it if anyone told him what it was. In any case images changed, and he urged that PEN should make war on images that were out of date or rapidly becoming so. The fact that the GDR protest was only a ritual gesture was made clear when Heinz Kamnitzer, having failed in his attempt to have Koestler removed from the programme, then asked Peter for an introduction to him.

The meeting of the Executive Committee included an amusing clash of swords between Leda Mileva and Peter. Mrs. Mileva, in her best headmistress fashion, said that, although she appreciated the brevity of Peter's Secretary's Report, she thought it would be better if it were entirely factual and did not include subjective comments such as those he had made on the Vienna Congress. Quite unfazed, Peter agreed that his Report was subjective and said he was afraid his Reports would continue to be so. He thought that perhaps Mrs. Mileva, in spite of her impressive command of the English language, had misunderstood his comment on the Vienna Congress ("If the meetings of the Executive were the stormiest ever, it is also true that the social events were among the most civilised; all the quarrels of the debating floor were forgotten outside the committee room".). This had been meant as a compliment to the delegates rather than the reverse.

6

It was not long before the London Congress that Kathleen von Simson came into our lives. An Englishwoman whose husband, Werner, was legal adviser to the West German PEN, she had for some time been doing voluntary work for writers in prison and when at the London Congress Michael Scammell (biographer of Solzhenitsyn and Editor of *Index on Censorship*) was elected Chairman of the Writers in Prison Committee, he stipulated that he would only take on the job if she continued as Corresponding Secretary of the Committee. She replied that she would only continue under an active Chairman. This was the beginning of a partnership which lasted for more than ten years. They formed an ideal combination, since she was an untiring backroom worker who would have hated to stand up in the International Executive and report on the WiPC's work, something which Michael did brilliantly. Kathleen's fierce dedication to the imprisoned and harassed writers whose cases she took up could be trying to those of us who were less dedicated. I had become used to a Writers in Prison Committee which consisted of two or three internationally known writers such as Rosamond Lehmann and Arthur Miller, whose chief function had been to put their names to telegrams composed by David and sent to Heads of State. This had involved no more work in the office than typing and sending off the telegrams. When Kathleen first appeared on the scene the WiPC had no office or staff of its own, so she had to make use of our services. Her technique was that of the iron hand within the velvet glove. "Dear Elizabeth, I know how busy you are, but I wonder if you could just . . .", or, when I answered the phone: "Dear Elizabeth, you do sound tired. I hate to add to your burdens, but it would be a great help if you could just . . ."! Needless to say, thus put on the spot, I always obliged. In return she was very generous with invitations to dinner at their flat in South Kensington, and even once gave my brother and sister-in-law and their four small children the use of a chalet by the lake at Interlaken for their summer holiday. The von Simson's main home was in Freiburg, but they also had a holiday house in Interlaken as well as their London flat. This style of living suited Werner, who liked the good things of life, but not Kathleen, who was of a far more ascetic temperament . She adored Werner, and therefore happily arranged dinner parties for him, but would herself have been content with bread and cheese in an attic. She took great pleasure in her children and grandchildren, but otherwise channelled all her energies into the defence and pastoral care of her adopted prisoners. The present work of the WiPC, with its own office and professional staff working in close cooperation with many of the PEN Centres, still owes a great debt to the amateur and voluntary beginnings made by Kathleen in 1976.

The way the issue of writers in prison was dealt with before Michael and Kathleen took over was exemplified by a resolution which the American Centre put forward at the London meeting, which, containing no names or details, simply expressed concern at the plight of writers in prison "because of their ideas and writings" and then listed over thirty countries all over the world which were guilty of imprisoning writers. Frankie Jose welcomed the resolution, but pointed out that writers were also human beings with family responsibilities and in some of the Third World countries named they had no choice but to jump when the authorities told them to. For this reason he pleaded for compassion and understanding for those who were silent or who acquiesced in the actions of totalitarian regimes. Coming from a man who kept a suitcase ready packed at his bookshop in Manila in case he should be arrested for his opposition to the Marcos regime, this comment carried particular force.

The London Congress marked the end of Victor Pritchett's term of office as International President, and the only person put up to succeed him was Mario Vargas Llosa, the Peruvian novelist, who was elected in absentia. To us Mario was a dark horse who had been put forward by the American Centre and whose work was not yet well-known in England. Fortunately his term of office coincided with his tenure of the Simon Bolivar Chair of Latin American Studies at Cambridge, so he was easily accessible from London. Since there was no Peruvian PEN Centre at that time, he was not even a member of PEN when he was elected, and probably knew as little about us as we knew about him, but he very swiftly remedied that and, because of his charm and intelligence, allied to striking good looks, had the delegates to the International Executive Committee eating out of his hand from his first meeting. Peter and I were to get to know him and his wife Patricia much better when we all went to Moscow together in May 1977 to hold discussions with the Soviet Writers' Union (as Arthur Miller and David Carver had done before us) on the possibility of establishing a Russian PEN Centre.

A very significant consequence of the London Congress, both for International PEN and English PEN, was Josephine's election as General Secretary of English PEN, which took place at the Centre's A.G.M. in December 1976. Ever since Peter had taken over from David as both International Secretary and Secretary of English PEN he had wanted to find someone else to take on the English Centre job, both in fairness to English PEN, which had always taken second place in David's affections, and to mark the fact that, although, for financial reasons, International PEN and English PEN shared premises, English PEN was only one of the many Centres all over the world and, although it had been the founder Centre, it no longer held a pre-eminent position. Because of the splendid way in which Josephine had organised the London Congress, she was obviously the best possible candidate for the secretaryship, and she was elected by acclamation. Enthusiasm for PEN was in her blood; her mother, the novelist Joanna Cannan, had been an early member.

7

To KEVIN FITZGERALD   *Hamburg*
Crossways, Chinnor, Oxon   *May, 1977*

Dear Kevin,
Disaster! One of my suitcases has got lost en route, and of course it's
the one which holds my clothes, not the one with the PEN documents.
I shall have to go to the Mayor's Reception tonight improperly dressed.
Whatever would David have said?!
   A lot of old friends here, but no-one from the Communist bloc
because they say that our hosts, the Writers in Exile Centre, will use
the Conference for anti-Communist propaganda. Don't repeat this,
but I expect they're right. Love, Elizabeth

The Vargas Llosas, Peter and I left for Moscow direct from the Writers
in Exile Centre Conference in Hamburg, the holding of which had
been confirmed by a vote of 19 to 8 at the London Congress, with 14
abstentions. The organisers of that Conference were an oddly assorted
couple: Gabriel Laub, a fat, bouncy and ebullient Czech exile, and
Bettina Vadasi, an elegant and ladylike Hungarian who had married
a German. Bettina treated Gabriel rather like a savage who needed to
be taught society manners; he amiably ignored her efforts. In spite of
their totally different personalities, they between them organised a very
efficient Conference. We stayed in the rather spartan surroundings of
a Catholic hostel which was in walking distance of the Hamburg
Conference Centre, and every day Bettina, teetering on her high heels,
led us in procession to the Conference Centre.
   My lost suitcase and the consequent threat that I might turn up at
the Mayor's Reception in the trouser suit I'd travelled in was a cause
of great concern to Bettina and to Marianne Kunvari (her fellow
Hungarian, a member of the London Branch of the Writers in Exile
Centre, who worked in our office and had come over to help with
the organisation of the Conference). Both dressed much more smartly
and elaborately than I have ever aspired to do, and I was uneasy when
they told me to meet them in the ladies' cloakroom of the hotel where
the party was to be held so that I could try on some of Bettina's dresses.

Fortunately all Bettina's dresses (like Ivana Tigrid's cheongsam) turned out to be two sizes too small for me. My suitcase turned up the next day.

The first evening Pavel invited me for a drink at the bar and, in the course of conversation, I mentioned the Moscow trip to him. The Centres had not yet been officially told about it because Peter and Mario reckoned that, since it was a purely exploratory visit, it did not require the sanction of the International Executive Committee. All Pavel's virulent anti-communist feelings were, however, immediately aroused as a result of my indiscretion, as well as his latent suspicions of Peter as a Left Wing sympathiser. He found an opportunity to raise the matter in the Committee and the discussion swiftly degenerated as both the main protagonists lost their tempers. Pavel got up and asked to be told the truth for a change. Peter said that Pavel had openly and publicly insulted him by calling him a liar. He had thought it better at this stage of very delicate negotiations not to make the Moscow trip an official PEN matter, although certainly not to keep it secret. He had told Tigrid this the previous day in confidence because he had then counted him as a friend and had not thought that Tigrid would take advantage of this confidence to mount a public attack upon him. Pavel denied that he had called Peter a liar and a lot of oil was poured on the troubled waters by many delegates, a vote of confidence in the International President and Secretary was carried, and the Moscow visit was unanimously approved. This was, however, the end of the uneasy friendship which had hitherto prevailed between Peter and Pavel.

*

It was a relief to get away from the tense atmosphere of the Hamburg Conference and drive off in a rented car to Bonn, where Mario and Patricia had to collect their Russian visas before we flew to Moscow. On the way we spent the night in the sort of simple but pleasant wayside inn in which I used to stay with my parents when we were driving on the Continent. "Peter", Mario said , when we came together for dinner, "Have you ever, *ever* stayed in such a terrible place – not counting when you were in the Army?"! I think he must have changed his view of it when we arrived at the Peking Hotel in Moscow, a comfortless barrack of a place dating from the days of Sino-Russian friendship.

When we landed at Moscow Airport we were greeted by Victor Rameses, who had been interpreter to the delegation of observers from the Soviet Writers' Union who had attended the London Congress the previous year. I knew that he had then become friendly with the

Pullein-Thompson sisters, so, for something to say, I mentioned that I had heard that Josephine's sister Diana and her husband Dennis Farr, Director of The Courtauld Institute, were also in Moscow, attending an International Council of Museums' meeting. I was considerably startled, immediately after we had checked into our hotel and while I was still gazing at the light fixtures in my large and gloomy room, wondering where the secret microphones might be hidden, to get a telephone call from Diana asking if I was all right. I do not know what Victor had said to her to arouse her concern, but I thought afterwards that if I had found myself in difficulties in Moscow, I could not think of anyone better to appeal to for help than a Pullein-Thompson. Undoubtedly all the forces of the KGB would not have prevailed against them. Fortunately such help did not prove necessary; we were very well looked after.

We had two interpreters attached to us: the English-speaking Alla for Peter and me; and the Spanish-speaking Yuri – a rather melancholy figure – for Mario and Patricia. Alla, who was the wife of a professor of Physics at Moscow University, was our principal guide, and it was she who , on our first evening, went through our projected programme with us. This, she told us, would include, in addition to a meeting and lunch with Gyorgy Markov, the First Secretary, and other officials of the Soviet Writers' Union, evenings at the Bolshoi Ballet and the Taganka Theatre, together, of course, with the obligatory visit to Lenin's tomb. We would also be taken to see some of the former churches, still preserved in The Kremlin. She asked us if this programme was to our liking, and was rather flustered when Mario, large-eyed like a small boy deprived of a Christmas treat, said he wanted to go to the circus. "Everywhere I go in the world I always go to the circus", he said. The programme was hastily amended to include a visit to the Moscow State Circus, which I found very exciting, particularly for its high wire acts, but which did not altogether satisfy Mario. He said it lacked the smell of the sawdust in the Big Top. We queue-jumped to get into Lenin's tomb – a curiously emotionless experience – and again to get into the Taganka Theatre to see Liubimov's production of Bulgakov's *The Master and Margarita*, which was playing to packed houses. We were even introduced to Liubimov in the interval, but unfortunately I was in no state to appreciate the honour. We had earlier that day had a long lunch at the Soviet Writers' Union, with many toasts and much vodka, and had then been taken to meet a pleasant youngish couple of intellectuals (obviously government-approved for presentation to foreigners) who had entertained us in their flat in one of the smarter Moscow apartment blocks and plied us with tea and rich chocolate cake. As a result, by the time we got to the theatre I had a raging headache and the very noisy production, full of loud bangs and flashing lights, finished me off so that I could not stick it out to the end and had to ask to be taken back to the hotel in the second interval.

It was a great privilege also to be given seats for the Bolshoi Ballet, and Alla, who escorted us there, would have been turned away at the door had not Peter, pretending that he was an invalid who needed her care and attention, bluffed the doorman into letting her through so that she enjoyed what was obviously for her the experience of a lifetime. The ballet concerned an unhappy love story in the unpromising setting of a hydro-electric plant somewhere in Siberia, but turned out nevertheless to be enchanting.

Those were the days when each floor of every Russian hotel was guarded by an elderly female dragon, who took our room keys from us when we went out and handed them back to us when we returned. Peter, with his usual resistance to authority, tried to circumvent our particular dragon and go out with his key in his pocket, but he was sternly called to order. Getting breakfast was another ordeal. There was no such thing as breakfast in the restaurant. Instead there was a small shop on each floor, where one could buy coffee and black bread from another dragon, who presided behind a counter, and then eat it standing up. Having no Russian, I could only point at what I wanted, and, since there was no butter or jam visible, I had to do without them.

For our other meals we were well looked after by our faithful guides, who took us to some of the best restaurants in Moscow, including one Mongolian one where the food was particularly delicious. On one fateful evening, however, Alla and Yuri took the evening off. We said airily that we would be quite all right. We would have dinner in our hotel. This proved to be far from easy, since, as for everything in Moscow in those days, there was a long queue to get into the dining-room. Seeing that there was a danger that we should not get any dinner, Peter boldly jumped the queue while the Vargas Llosas and I lurked shamefacedly in the background. Having got into the dining room and got a menu, our troubles were not over, however, because we could not read the menu and were in any case totally ignored by the waiters. Here too Peter came to our rescue, whilst we tried to pretend that he was nothing to do with us. He stood up, flapped his arms and made a noise like a hen which had just laid an egg. This eccentric behaviour by a doubtless mad capitalist foreigner, who must obviously be fed and got out of the dining room as soon as possible, brought waiters scurrying from every direction, and we had eggs for our supper.

Our discussions with the Soviet Writers' Union came to nothing, as all such discussions had in the past. One of the stumbling blocks was the existence of "Estonian" and "Latvian" PEN Centres. These Centres dated from the time when Estonia and Latvia were independent countries, but, since their membership now consisted of Estonian and Latvian writers living in exile, Gyorgy Markov said that they should be renamed to take account of this fact. Peter replied that if Russian writers wished to apply to join International PEN, they were welcome to do so, but there could be no question of PEN changing its constitution to accommodate them. More basic was the stipulation in the Charter that members must oppose "any form of suppression of freedom of expression in the country and community to which they belong". It was not until the Gorbachev era that Russian writers could subscribe to this clause, so it was not until 1989 that a Russian PEN Centre was elected.

Whether or not our visit, and all the uproar that it caused in Hamburg, and later that year at the Sydney Congress, was worthwhile, I rather doubt, but I'm afraid I quelled any scruples I had about that and about accepting hospitality from the fat cats of the Board of The Soviet Writers' Union, and thoroughly enjoyed the unusual opportunities it afforded me. In the course of our visit I got to know Alla quite well and she confided in me that her marriage was unhappy and her husband would insist on bringing his graduate students back to their tiny flat, so that she was condemned to do her writing in the kitchen. She spoke nostalgically of a conference somewhere in the provinces the previous year which Victor Rameses had also attended, and I caught the whiff of a frustrated love affair. One day when she came to collect us for an excursion the others were not ready so I asked her to come and wait in my room. It was not until she was coming through the door that I remembered that the paperback by my bedside was a spy thriller in which the Russians were the villains, and the rather lurid cover made this plain. I hastily turned it over, but not before she had spotted it and grabbed it enthusiastically, saying that she loved spy thrillers. When we parted she asked me if I would send her some paperbacks from London. She said that the parcel was more likely to reach her if I addressed it to her care of The Soviet Writers' Union. I duly did that, but never heard from her that she had received it, so I am afraid my carefully chosen John Le Carres and Len Deightons may have ended up on the bookshelves of some KGB agent, who would no doubt have found them absorbing reading.

8

Extract from letter from   Chinnor
KEVIN FITZGERALD   September 1977

*". . . How are you all in your new quarters? You of course are hardly
ever there as you rush round the world placating poets, chatting up
Chinese, and getting writers out of gaols . . ."*

Whilst all these excitements were taking place abroad, our base in
Chelsea was no longer secure. The lease on Glebe House had expired
in 1974 and, since PEN could not afford to renew it, we had had
reluctantly to let that beautiful house fall into the hands of developers.
This, although sad, had had the advantage that the developers had
immediately started work on restoring the fabric, which was much in
need of it (we had become accustomed to using wastepaper bins to
catch the drips from the office ceiling on wet days), and it had even
seemed at first that we might be able to retain a foothold in the
building. It had soon become apparent, however, that there would
not be enough space for us at a rent we could afford. Also, as we had
never complied with the requirements of our full repairing lease, we
would be faced with a bill for dilapidations running into thousands
of pounds, so the English PEN Committee had welcomed an approach
from the Chelsea Arts Club. The Club was in financial difficulties
because of a dwindling membership, and it had seemed that to offer
PEN the rental as offices of two of the bedrooms in their charming
house in Old Church Street, as well as getting some revenue from
PEN members' spending in the bar and restaurant, might be the answer
to their problems. The proposal was attractive to PEN because,
although the offices would be very pokey, the membership would have
a free run of the bar, restaurant and billiard room, as well as the very
pleasant garden, and would also have the possibility of staying in the
Club at a very cheap rate. The next best thing to David's Project for
a Writers' House.

Peter reported all this to the Hamburg meeting, explaining that a
final decision hung on the Chelsea Arts Club's A.G.M. at the end of
May. Sadly, at that meeting the Arts Club's membership rebelled at

the idea of their premises being flooded with PEN members who would be paying a much lower rate of subscription than they were, so we were once more in danger of being out on the street – but not for long.

Our saviours appeared in the persons of Donald Blake and John Seabrook, of The London Sketch Club, who were also members of the Chelsea Arts Club so had been privy to all the negotiations between us and the Chelsea Arts. The Sketch Club was another old and prestigious association, which dated from the Victorian era and still smacked of the Edwardian. Like the Chelsea Arts they owned their own premises (7 Dilke Street), but had a cash flow problem. They could not offer us a garden or bedrooms, since their premises backed directly onto a larger house on the Embankment (for which it had formerly been the stables) and consisted only of two smallish offices, an antiquated kitchen and ladies' and gents' lavatories on the ground floor, and a large studio and a small bar on the upper floor. They did, however, offer us the offices at a rent we could afford, together with use of the studio and bar on Wednesday evenings for meetings of English PEN. Best of all, they were prepared to welcome us with open arms. This was more than we could have hoped for, and we jumped at the offer.

So a hot summer weekend in August 1977 found Josephine and me, in our oldest clothes, supervising the move from Glebe House of all PEN's furniture, office equipment and files. Josephine had enlisted the services of an Irish carpenter called Mr. Lynch to put up shelves, taking care to show him the box files which the shelves in the front office would have to support. These contained all the Congress records and so were quite heavy. The removers having done their work, Mr. Lynch was busy in the back office at Dilke Street whilst we arranged the box files on the shelves he had already erected in the front office. Being taller than Josephine, I had the job of standing on a desk and putting the boxes in place as she handed them up to me. This was a dusty occupation, but otherwise quite satisfying to my orderly mind. The work progressed well and we both gave cries of triumph as I put the last box in place. Our triumph was short-lived. There was a nasty rending noise, followed by a crash as the whole edifice of shelves and boxes folded in on itself and collapsed like a house of cards. Fortunately it fell downwards and not sideways, so I was able to jump clear. Mr. Lynch, hastily summoned by Josephine from the back office to view the resulting scene of devastation, was greatly distressed. "Sure, it was a total misunderstanding!", he exclaimed, going on to explain that since she had shown him an empty box file it had been on that basis that he had calculated the weight the shelves would have to bear! He replaced the shelves, with metal brackets to support them, and the box files are still in position twenty years later. He also strengthened the shelves he had erected in the back office, since they had to bear the weight of a bust of PEN's first President, John Galsworthy, and he was clearly haunted by visions of that crashing down on someone's head.

Dilke Street was too remote from public transport to be ideal for the members, but it was a very welcoming haven for us. Peter and Josephine amicably shared the back office, which also, with a rearrangement of desks and chairs, served as a dining room where Josephine entertained the speakers to supper on Wednesday nights. The front office served as the general office for both International and English PEN, who also shared my services and those of Bill Barazetti, who continued to do the accounts for both organisations. He had hated the upheaval of the move ("like an old dog being given a new basket", as Josephine said), but was pacified by having his disreputable old desk transported from Glebe House to a corner of the Dilke Street office. The little Hungarian exile, Marianne Kunvari, who, as a member of English PEN, had joined our staff as a volunteer for the London Congress and had stayed on to do the clerical work and filing, in spite of her age and frail health devotedly trekked down from St. John's Wood twice a week, whatever the weather, and rustled about amongst the Congress boxes ("like a mad mouse", in Josephine's phrase), apologising with every other breath, for any disturbance she was causing. Josephine's letters were typed by Margaret Grant, a tough elderly Scotswoman, strong-minded and rather deaf. She was the only person who had the temerity to call Josephine "Jo", and seemed quite unaware that this was not a popular move. She also, having had a long and distinguished career in the civil service before she officially retired, was convinced that she knew in advance what Josephine was going to say in her letters. She was not always right, and high decibel protests could often be heard emanating from the back office as Josephine tried to get through to Margaret the fact that what she wanted to say differed from what Margaret thought she wanted to say.

The Sketch Club continued to make us feel welcome. Being an all-male institution, they nevertheless valued "the woman's touch", as they quaintly said. More to the point, we were there to perform the invaluable task of taking in the weekly beer delivery. They themselves were only at Dilke Street on two evenings a week: on Tuesdays for a life class (when they took it in turns to cook their own dinners), and on Fridays, when they had a proper cook. The Friday dinner, which was a meat and two veg. affair followed by a solid pudding, was very convivial and there were usually guests from the world of entertainment to perform songs to the piano. It always ended with a spirited rendering of "Watchman, what of the night?". Once or twice Josephine and I were invited to a Ladies' Night. On these occasions the jokes, the Sketchers assured us, were toned down so as not to shock our finer sensibilities. One Friday night when I was working late with a visiting Catalan translator, kind John Seabrook invited me and the translator to have a drink in the bar. It was not a Ladies' Night, so I should not really have shown my face upstairs, but John said it would be all right because the members had gone in to the studio for dinner. Since the hatch between the bar and the studio was raised the Catalan was able to get a flavour of the occasion whilst he drank his glass of wine. He was understandably astonished and bemused. "Only in England could this happen," he exclaimed.

9

to KEVIN FITZGERALD   *Sydney*
Crossways, Chinnor, Oxon   *December 1977*

Dear Kevin,
*Mario and Peter and I stopped off for an Asian Writers' Conference
in The Philippines on the way here. The atmosphere in Manila is
very different from 1970. No question this time of being received at
Malacanang Palace or getting free helicopter rides! Frankie Jose and
his friends are brave and funny and constantly make jokes at the
expense of Imelda Marcos, even in public places. No earthquakes this
time, but it was a relief to come on to the hot dry sunshine here after
the humidity in Manila. Much love, Elizabeth*

The small PEN Centre in Sydney did a magnificent job as hosts to the
1977 Congress and arranged splendid parties for us, including one at
the Opera House. I fell in love with Sydney's spectactular harbour
and vibrant atmosphere and found the Australians warm and welcoming, with a pleasantly relaxed attitude to life.

The atmosphere in the International Executive Committee, however, was far from relaxed and was hot rather than warm, since the
discussion in Hamburg and our subsequent visit to Moscow had given
rise to a bevy of statements by various individuals and Centres for and
against a possible Soviet PEN. These had been circulated in advance of
the Congress so that delegates had come to Sydney in battle array.

After heated debate Francis King put the situation in perspective
by pointing out that since no application had been received from
writers in the Soviet Union, the present discussion was as if a scientific
conference were to spend time considering what to do when the
Martians landed. Nina Puyet, a large and opulent lady from Manila,
who had formed a great attachment for Francis, whom she had been
trying to induce to come to The Philippines to write in her beachside
hut, concluded the debate by making an emotional appeal that no
Russian writer should be prevented from joining PEN. "It is better to
light a candle than to curse the dark", she quoted rather cryptically.
The discussion concluded with general agreement that the issue of a

Russian PEN Centre was dead for the moment, but that contacts with individual Russian writers should be pursued.

As in Hamburg, the distressing part of the debate from my point of view was the duel between Pavel and Peter, both close friends of mine, but now bitterly opposed. Still upset by their quarrel, I found myself when the meeting broke up travelling up in the lift with Ivana Tigrid, who, with her usual friendly generosity, pressed a bottle of duty free gin upon me. I said that I could not possibly accept such a present from her after what had taken place between Pavel and Peter in the Executive Committee. Since Ivana had not been present in the Committee meeting, she must have been astonished by my emotional reaction and I regretted it afterwards because she was an innocent bystander and it meant the end of another friendship which I had valued.

Ironically, when, on a free afternoon, Peter and I were waiting on the quayside to get the ferry across to the Zoo, who should appear at the end of the jetty but the Tigrids. Since we were the only four people on that particular ferry we could not absolutely ignore each other, but our greetings were very distant. When we disembarked at the Zoo we carefully went off in different directions. Peter added to my anxieties by ignoring all the forbidding notices and climbing into the koala bear enclosure to take a close-up picture of them. The koalas sensibly ignored him and no irate zoo official appeared to remonstrate with him, so I enjoyed the rest of our visit. There was no sign of the Tigrids on our return ferry.

It was not until seventeen years later, when Peter and I were in Prague for the 1994 Congress and Pavel (now back home as Vaclav Havel's Minister of Culture) whisked us off from the official Closing Ceremony to lunch in his and Ivana's spartan flat overlooking the old Jewish cemetery that the two old men (both nearly eighty) made up their differences. Even then, I felt that if we had stayed on too long after lunch hostilities might have been resumed!

It was at the Sydney Congress that Miss Moh, as a reward for all that she had done to activate the Korean Centre, was elected an International Vice-President. To celebrate this she summoned the Korean Ambassador from Canberra to give a dinner party for the International President, the International Secretary and one or two other guests in a private room in one of the smarter Sydney hotels. I was included and found myself sitting opposite Mario. The first course was oysters, which Mario, not wishing to offend his host, foolhardily ate in spite of being allergic to them. The result was dramatic. I've never seen anyone so quickly turn such a spectacular shade of green! Heroically he continued with the meal and, when the microphone was pushed towards him at the end, made an impeccable speech of thanks to our hosts before asking to be excused. He managed to make it back to the Congress hotel before being violently sick, which luckily got the poison out of his system so that by the next day he had recovered.

The post-Congress tour was a four-day visit to the other Australian PEN Centre, in Melbourne. Josephine and I went via Canberra, travelling by bus to join Mario and Peter, who had flown on ahead. We felt that we gained considerable kudos from having two such personable men waiting to meet us at the bus station!

We all took a bus tour of the capital, but disliked its artificiality and lack of human scale. It's a car city with no little corner shops anywhere. The most striking feature of this immaculately symmetrical city is Lake Burley Griffin, and the photograph I took of Josephine and Mario in conversation beside it was published in the next issue of the PEN Broadsheet to illustrate Josephine's account of the Sydney Congress.

It was a relief to get to Melbourne, even though it seemed rather staid and stuffy in comparison with Sydney. The Secretary of the Melbourne PEN Centre, Jean Gittins, kindly put Josephine and me up in her large apartment in Domain Park. She had been born in Hong Kong, of Anglo-Chinese extraction. Since her father was very wealthy she had been brought up in luxury in the exclusive residential district of The Peak. She and her two young children had survived great privations in Stanley Camp during the war. They had come to Australia, expecting to be reunited with Jean's husband, Billy, but, tragically, he had died in internment in Japan. Jean had therefore had to make a life for herself and her children in Australia. Her account of all this had been published as *Eastern Windows – Western Skies* and she presented Josephine and me with a copy. I found this a fascinating and moving book, but there was one passage which struck a particular chord with us. This was her description of how the Hong Kong traffic police had lain in wait for her and finally, in spite of her father's importance, clapped a fine upon her for dangerous driving. Even in Melbourne she drove in the middle of the road as if she were alone on The Peak, and when she offered to take any of us in her car there was an undignified scramble to avoid sitting in the front seat.

Jean's apartment was air-conditioned, but outside the December sun blazed down. In the Botanical Gardens, which are the most spectacular sight in Melbourne, we kept as far as possible in the shade of the great trees, whilst admiring the profusion of dazzling blossom. Some of our colleagues on the post-Congress tour had come without proper protection against the sun, and Josephine did her bit for international relations by plastering sun block on the noses of the German delegation.

On the last evening we were taken to Monsalvat, a pseudo medi-aeval manor some way outside the city which had been built before the Second World War for a commune of writers and artists presided over by a patriarchal painter, a sort of Australian Augustus John, called Jurgens. The original occupants had gone, but it was still used as a craft centre. We dined in the refectory and then wandered out into the bush to gaze up at the stars. The Southern Cross did not stand out from amongst the other brilliant stars as I had expected, and even our hosts argued as to which constellation it was. Peter afterwards said, typically, that he had known all the time which it was, but thought it tactless to say so. When I later read Francis's chilling novel "Act of Darkness" I found Monsalvat recreated there, unmistakable although under a different name.

Whilst the Sydney Congress was in progress a bush fire had been raging in the Blue Mountains, a short drive north west of the city, so the Christmas which Josephine and I spent there after all the other participants had departed was not quite as we had planned it. Instead of the blue haze of eucalyptus vapour which gives these beautiful hills their name, there was the blackness of miles of scorched gum trees. We did manage, however, to find an unspoilt area to walk in and eat our picnic lunch, to which our hotel had kindly added some Christmas cake. The weather was hot, but overcast, so I did not take as much care as I should have done to protect my face. The boiled lobster effect was even worse than the sunburn I had acquired in Ceylon. Everywhere we went thereafter I had to get used to the uninhibited curiosity of the Australians: "Oooh, whatever happened to your face?"!

To see as much of Australia as we could in the short time available to us we had decided to travel by bus up to Cairns. We realised that we should need to stop off somewhere on the way, but the travel agent in Brisbane with whom we made our booking seemed to know as little about the country to the north as we did, so we ended up by choosing at random a place on the coast called Gladstone. We set off from Brisbane on New Year's Eve and, in spite of the fact that the bus carried a stern warning against drinking or taking drugs, there was one noisy reveller on board who had obviously started his celebrations early. We wondered how the driver, who was alone in charge of thirty or more passengers, would cope with this disruption. He did so with admirable economy and effect. He simply stopped the bus by the roadside, walked back down the vehicle, removed the beer bottle from the hand of the startled drunk, saying: "That's enough of that, mate", dropped the bottle in a convenient litter bin, and drove on. This increased our respect for Australian bus drivers, who wear uniforms like airline pilots (only with shorts) and wield a similar unquestioned authority. The only time I saw one of them slightly shaken was when Josephine and I were picked up from Gladstone after our twenty-hour stop-off there. Since it was the early hours of the morning and we were the only passengers waiting at the bus stop we were relieved to see our bus and Josephine said to the driver as he loaded our suitcases into the luggage compartment: "We regard Australian bus drivers as father figures". The driver, who was probably in his thirties, looked slightly askance at the two rather unkempt middle-aged English ladies who were boarding his bus in the middle of the night, and replied smartly: "We prefer to regard ourselves as great lovers!".

Gladstone had turned out to be an aluminium smelting town and not, on the face of it, a desirable tourist spot. However, we struck lucky because we found from a leaflet in our motel bedroom that there was an island in the harbour to which there were boat trips. This turned out to be an enterprise run by a young English couple from Newcastle, who not only ran the boat to and from the island, but also, for an all-in charge, provided lunch (steak and salad) by the pool and a bumpy ride round the island on a trailer towed by a tractor. Our fellow passengers were also Geordies who were in some way related to the young couple, so we spent the day swimming and lazing in a transplanted Tyneside atmosphere.

At Cairns we only stayed one night at the motel the Brisbane travel agent had booked us in at because we found that the hairy yellow carpet which clothed the walls of our bedroom as well as the floor was the home for a family of large cockroaches of a matching yellow colour. We tried trapping them under tooth glasses, but found our supply of glasses was inadequate. We moved out the next day to a much pleasanter lodging down by the harbour. From then on our visit to Cairns was idyllic. We went to the local cinema, where "Picnic at Hanging Rock" was showing, and found ourselves sitting in deck chairs in a sort of village hall. We went on a tour to the Atherton Tableland and walked in the rain forest, keeping a keen eye out for venomous snakes, but only meeting a tame emu which was attached to the restaurant where we had lunch. Like Jean Paget and her Joe in *A Town Like Alice* we took the boat trip to Green Island to get a glimpse of the marvels of the Great Barrier Reef. There we had lunch on the beach and went down into the underwater observatory, a glass dome where the human visitors seemed to provide a never-ending source of entertainment to the shoals of marvellously variegated fish which swam up to peer in at us.

When the time came for us to return to Sydney we flew as far as Brisbane. Even our admiration for the drivers could not compensate for the discomforts of bus travel, particularly at night, when we always seemed to be seated just at the point where there was an inconspicuous step in the aisle which other passengers en route for the lavatory or the water tap at the back of the bus invariably fell up or down, making a grab for the nearest handhold, which often turned out to be the head of whichever of us was sitting on the aisle seat. The short haircuts which we had both had in preparation for our Australian travels stood up quite well to this treatment, but it was not conducive to peaceful slumbers.

Back in Sydney we were the guests of Stella and Jerry Wilkes in their apartment overlooking Darling Harbour. I had known Stella years before when she was a BBC producer and Organiser of the Radio Features Department headed by Laurence Gilliam. I was working at the time as secretary to Giles Cooper, who, although he also wrote for the stage and for television, was best known as a radio dramatist. Stella and I had met again, to our mutual surprise and pleasure, when she visited Glebe House as Treasurer of the Sydney PEN Centre and she told me the romantic story of how, as a successful career woman in her forties, she came to marry Jerry Wilkes, an English journalist living in Australia. By a strange coincidence their letters of condolence to each other on the death of a mutual close friend had been written on the same day and had crossed in the post. When, later, Jerry came to England they had met and fallen in love. Eventually Jerry returned to Australia, where Stella joined him on secondment from the BBC He had been insistent in asking her to marry him, but she had been very hesitant to abandon her career and all her friends in London, so a trial period on the other side of the world had seemed a wise move. After fascinating months exploring the continent with Jerry and making programmes for the BBC, she had returned to London only long enough to resign her job and had then settled happily with him in Sydney, where she became active both in broadcasting and in the PEN Centre.

Thus it was that Josephine and I came to be enjoying the Wilkes' hospitality for two nights and swimming with them within the protection of a shark net at the harbour beach in Neilsen Park just before catching our plane back to fog-bound and snow-bound January in England.

My neighbour on the journey home, a girl who boarded the plane at Singapore, was evidently ill, immediately wrapping herself in her blanket and refusing all food and drink. I had a lot of opportunity to inhale her germs because when we thought we had reached the end of our journey we were turned away from Heathrow and spent some time on the tarmac at Manchester Airport, waiting for the fog over London to clear. Since the airport buildings were already overcrowded with the passengers from other diverted flights, we had to stay on the plane, whilst the toilets became blocked and stinking. Eventually we landed at Heathrow, by which time our ankles were so swollen that we could not get our shoes on, but had to leave the plane in a freezing temperature, with snow on the ground, wearing the sandals in which we had boarded the plane in the far different climate of Sydney. Not surprisingly, I went down with flu soon after my return home and my golden memories of Australia were temporarily forgotten.

*

Whilst Josephine and I were enjoying the Australian sunshine, the presidium of PEN had dispersed in different directions. Mario had gone on round the world to visit the Centres in Hong Kong, Taiwan and Bangkok, whilst Peter had spent Christmas in New Zealand, then gone on to Santiago, Lima and Bogota on PEN business, before meeting up with Barbara in California, and driving with her to Mexico and then to New York. He was away for nearly four months, but was conscientious in putting through a weekly phone call to the office. In addition Mario was still based in Cambridge, so I could always consult him about any problems that arose. I was nevertheless depressed by Peter's prolonged absence and thought it was time I made a break from PEN. The trouble was that I felt that I had become such a specialist in the affairs of PEN that I was ill-equipped to work for any other organisation. In any case I could hardly give in my notice over a long distance telephone line, and by the time Peter returned we were already in the throes of preparing for the Stockholm Congress.

10

To KEVIN FITZGERALD
Crossways, Chinnor, Oxon

Stockholm
May 1978

Dear Kevin,
I am of course staying at the best hotel in Stockholm, the Grand,
beautifully situated down by the harbour. Since Josephine is only an
unofficial delegate she's co-habiting in a much more modest establish-
ment with Kate Nott and Michael Rubinstein. She complains that
Kate has drunk large quantities of her (J's) duty free Scotch to cure
a heavy cold, which J. has now caught. Michael makes puns at break-
fast – never J's best time! Much love, Elizabeth

The English Centre's official delegates at the Stockholm Congres were:
their President, the novelist Lettice Cooper, and the distinguished
biographer Jasper Ridley, both of whom were regarded by the other
delegates with a respect which was tinged with amusement. Lettice,
who was by then in her seventies although still very active, was a
cosy granny figure, her exterior belying the tough Yorkshire fibre and
shrewd intelligence which lay beneath. Jasper's prematurely white hair
and round rosy face gave him a Dickensian appearance, which was
enhanced by his habit of carrying a rolled black umbrella although
Stockholm's many inlets and waterways were sparkling in the May
sunshine

Amidst much serious discussion, although conducted with less ran-
cour than at some earlier meetings, a lighter note was introduced into
the meeting during Peter's report on inactive Centres. He reminded
the delegates that in Sydney the Colombian Centre had been declared
defunct because nothing had been heard from it. He had discovered
during his travels round Latin America after the Sydney Congress that
the Centre was far from being defunct. It was indeed active and its
Secretary, Hernando Torres Neira, was present in Stockholm to prove
it. Senor Torres Neira, a stout, bespectacled figure then came to the
rostrum, to general applause, raising his clasped arms above his head
in a victory salute. Unfortunately he had very little English so was
not able to capitalise on this propitious moment.

John Peet, as Press Officer, was quartered with us at the Grand Hotel, which was also where the Welcome Party was held. He turned up to this rather informally dressed and explained that when he unpacked the suit which he had brought with him for just this sort of occasion he found that his wife (whom he was just about to abandon for another woman) had taken her revenge by slashing it to pieces.

There were other delightful social occasions, the best of which was a splendid buffet in the Town Hall, followed by a visit to the enchanting eighteenth century Drottningholm Court Theatre, where we were treated to a Mozart concert given by musicians in the costume of the period. Swedish PEN made the inspired choice of Carlos de Radzitzky, our Belgian baron, to present a bouquet to the soprano at the end of the evening. He loved this and did it with a style appropriate to the setting.

On the last day we were taken for a cruise through the Archipelago. For a wonder the weather stayed fine so we were able to bask on deck whilst enjoying the scenery. I happened to be standing behind one of the ship's funnels to get the best view when I became aware that the historical and romantic novelist Rona Randall and one of the Scandinavian delegates were trading complaints about Peter. I cannot remember what their grievances were. Possibly Peter had not sufficiently concealed his disapproval when, at a drinks party which he gave for the English delegation, Rona had breached PEN's conventions and handed out publicity for her latest novel – or it may have been some more long-standing grudge. With foreign delegates he was generally popular and if he made a mistake he was always ready to apologise for it, but on the other hand he never minced his words if he felt it necessary to rebuke someone for their behaviour. I started by only half-listening to the malcontents' conversation, and by the time I had gathered its drift, it seemed too late to emerge dramatically from my hiding place and challenge them, so I remained, unheroically, lurking and fuming until they went away. It was on returning from this excursion to the Grand Hotel to make a quick change for dinner with Peter, John Paxton and Nancy that I got stuck in the cheongsam which Nancy had brought for me and which turned out to have been made to Ivana Tigrid's svelte measurements. Fortunately the Chinese tailor's stitches were so strong that they held in spite of all my struggles, and I was able to pass the dress on to Ivana as a peace offering when we next met.

*

Back at Dilke Street Margaret Grant left us, having inherited enough money to allow her to pursue her other interests (such as attending trials at the Old Bailey) without the interruption of coming to PEN and advising Josephine on her correspondence.

She was succeeded for a short time by a young army wife called Sally Berry. She and her husband, a colonel in the Green Jackets, and their small son, Nicholas, were quartered, conveniently near to PEN, in a flat in the Governor's wing of the Royal Hospital. Her husband had recently done a tour of duty in Ulster, and I remember her telephoning him one day to ask whether a small box with some wires sticking out of it which she had never before noticed on her car was meant to be there. To her embarrassment, it turned out to be some vital part of the mechanism, but obviously she had been well drilled to take no risks with possible bombs. She was a very pleasant addition to the staff – attractive and intelligent. Thanks to her, I was for once able to enjoy the Chelsea Flower Show, usually a nightmare, with all the parking spaces around Dilke Street occupied from early in the morning until late in the evening and fierce cohorts of tweed-clad gardeners up from the country for the day elbowing everyone else off the pavements in Royal Hospital Road. Thanks to Sally's privileged situation as a resident of The Royal Hospital, she was able to invite me (courtesy of the Governor) to a preview of the Show on the evening before it was opened to anyone else. It was marvellous to be able to wander peacefully round the displays without having to crane over and round other people.

Sadly, Sally's husband was soon transferred elsewhere. We advertised for a replacement for Sally and got loyal but scatter-brained Zena Kerridge. Zena stayed with PEN for many years – in fact until long after Peter and I had moved the International PEN office to Covent Garden in 1981. She evidently enjoyed the friendly and informal atmosphere at the PEN office and the social life – a summer party in Josephine's garden and a Christmas lunch at my house – as well as being able to exercise her shorthand, of which she was very proud. Zena's husband, Stan, a very handsome and sweet-natured man, was also drawn into the PEN family. He was a talented amateur artist and was useful in painting banners for us when we mounted protests outside embassies. The Kerridges lived in a flat in Chelsea Manor Street so Zena was able to get to the office first in the morning and open the post before the rest of us arrived. This was not always an advantage since letters from famous writers, of great archive value, occasionally got accidentally slit in half (until Josephine confiscated all the paper knives). Josephine ruefully said that she felt like Zena's secretary, rather than the other way round, because it was she who always had to look up addresses for Zena whilst she was poring over her shorthand outlines, determined to read them back accurately rather than trying to make sense of the letter she was typing. Whatever her deficiencies as a secretary, she was very good-natured and became much attached to the job – so much so that she was hurt and resentful when Josephine eventually had to ask her to leave. She was already well past retiring age and was unwilling even to try to grapple with the Amstrads which had replaced the battered typewriters, so there was no question but that she had to go. Josephine made her parting as pleasant as possible, giving a leaving party for her at which Antonia Fraser, as President of English PEN, made a speech and a presentation. Josephine and I both still receive Christmas and birthday cards from Zena to remind us that she is the conscientious keeper of a birthday book. She was succeeded by Tom Aitken, a writer and member of English PEN, who was well-acquainted with computers, and who was glad of the job because the brass band magazine he had been editing had just folded. His advent marked the end of the age of the shorthand typist at PEN.

But I've skipped over ten years and must go back to 1978, when the Stockholm Congress was followed by a very successful International Conference in Barcelona in October.

*

To KEVIN FITZGERALD   *Barcelona*
Crossways, Chinnor, Oxon   *October 1978*

Dear Kevin,
Greetings from the Ramblas. We're here for a PEN/Unesco Seminar on the sort of theme Unesco loves: "The Survival and Encouragement of Literature in Present-Day Society". Hans Magnus Enzensberger has sensibly said that Literature will survive if enough people enjoy it. End of discussion you might have thought, but alas no! Fortunately our Catalan hosts are laying on some good parties and of course there are plenty of good restaurants in the old town. Much love, Elizabeth

---

One of the speakers at the Barcelona Seminar was Amos Oz, and it is to Amos that I owe one of my most intriguing memories of this or any PEN meeting.

Lunch for the speakers and for the PEN staff was provided between sessions in a small dining room at the Institute, where round tables were laid for eight. When I went in on the first day Peter waved to me to join him and Barbara and Sukey. They already had with them the Saudi Arabian poet Abdullah M. Zaid, who was one of the guest speakers, together with his brother and Leda Mileva. When Amos Oz entered the room he glanced round for somewhere to sit and I saw a spark of mischief come into his eye when he saw the Zaids . He came over to us and asked Peter if he might take the vacant place at our table. The Saudis clearly had no idea who he was and, since he was fair-complexioned and blue-eyed, they probably took him for a European. Conversation round the table was general, if not particularly animated, and after a while Amos said something in Arabic. The Zaids were astonished, and one of them said: "Do you come from our part of the world?". "Yes, I'm a neighbour of yours," Amos replied, and then, in a throw away manner: "from Israel in fact". There was what seemed to me a long pause, during which I wondered whether the Zaids would refuse to remain at the same table as an Israeli. Peter said afterwards that, since they were seated between Barbara and Sukey and himself, he was sure that their tradition of the good manners incumbent upon a guest towards his host would prevent them from doing any such thing. Sure enough, he was right. They behaved as if Amos had not spoken and continued with their meal. General conversation was resumed and in the course of it the Zaids did exchange a few polite remarks with Amos. Since it was a time when, as so often, Israelis and Arabs were not officially on speaking terms, this seemed to me a small, but significant illustration of what PEN could achieve where governments failed.

John Peet was assisted as Press Officer in Barcelona by the Argentinian/Scottish writer and journalist Andrew Graham-Yooll, a member of English PEN, who, since he was bilingual in English and Spanish, was very well-qualified to deal with the Spanish press and so obtained a record amount of coverage for the Unesco Seminar. Andrew was much younger than John, who, like Peter, had been in Spain at the time of the Civil War, but they made a good team (their beards making them a sort of matched pair) and seemed to enjoy themselves. The press coverage pleased Alex Blokh greatly since he could take the cuttings back to Unesco Headquarters as proof of the success of his brainchild, which the Seminar was. He himself took a very active part, chairing one of the sessions as well as speaking. Possibly it was then that Peter, who had been looking around for a suitable successor ever since he himself had reluctantly succeeded David, set his sights on Alex.

Our Catalan hosts were very excited to learn that when Peter had come to Spain in 1936 as a volunteer to fight in the Civil War he had been imprisoned in the Citadel on Montjuic. Ironically this had been done by the government for whom he had come to fight, but who misguidedly suspected him of being a spy sent by the British Communist Party – almost as bad a crime in their eyes as fighting for General Franco. One of the most trying duties of the International Secretary is to make polite speeches to the hosts of official receptions, sometimes without much warning. Peter was always very good at this, being adept at thinking on his feet. In Barcelona, when we were received at the Palau de la Generalitat, the seat of government of Catalonia, he had no difficulty in finding something appropriate to say. He was able to point, with a dramatic gesture, up to Montjuic, and contrast the lavish hospitality we were receiving that evening from the Catalan authorities with the weeks he had spent on Montjuic, seeing his fellow prisoners (young Catholics for the most part) taken out and shot in the courtyard of the prison.

After Peter had made his speech I wandered off into a beautiful upper courtyard, ornamented with orange trees in tubs – I think, from consulting my guide book, that this must have been the Pati dels Tarongers – where I found myself having a rather sentimental conversation with Henryk Keisch, who, being the most ardent exponent of the virtues of the German Democratic Republic, was most people's least favourite delegate, but whom I rather admired for the evidently genuine fervour with which he presented his unpopular views. In any case I always felt that it was part of my job, as a member of the Secretariat, to befriend those delegates who were being shunned by their fellows – rather like a good hostess at a party. In those Cold War days the one most in need of befriending was Keisch. The other East Europeans, particularly the Hungarians, were better able to sink their political views and engage in social and literary chat – Ivan Boldizsar enjoyed telling anti-Russian jokes, and Laszlo Kery was a Shakespearian expert. Leda Mileva also, though not noted for her sense of humour, was adept socially. Whilst I was fraternising with Keisch, she was studying the royal portraits on the walls of the main gallery whilst Josephine teased her by expatiating on the attractions of monarchical government. Keisch also lacked a sense of humour and had the further disadvantage of not speaking English. (Just as Heinz Kamnitzer had acquired his fluency in English from spending the Second World War in London, so Keisch had spent the War in France, so his second language was French.) Although French was – and remains – one of PEN's two official languages I never, to my shame, achieved conversational fluency in it. However, Keisch evidently appreciated my stumbling efforts. I still have a rather pretty necklace of green beads which he gave me, either on this or a later occasion. He died of a heart attack some years later, perhaps fortunately for him before the GDR collapsed with the fall of the Berlin Wall.

Mario chaired the International Executive Committee which followed the Seminar with his usual charm and firmness. The most significant decision taken from my point of view was the vote to raise the international dues so as not only to pay Peter a token salary (£3000) – up to now he had done the job for only basic expenses – but also to pay me an extra £250 a year so that I could invest in a private pension. I owed this partly to Thilo Koch, but also to Werner von Simson (Kathleen's husband) – a persuasive speaker who painted an affecting picture of the impoverished old age which I should be facing if the Executive took no action to save me.

The Secretary of the Catalan PEN Centre was the well-known cartoonist Avelli Artis-Gener. He was a delightful man, but middle-aged and decidedly plain (I seem to remember that he had a glass eye) , so that Mario was astonished and greatly amused when, finding Avelli in the early hours of the morning leaning against a lamp-post in the last stages of exhaustion, he extracted from him an account of how a man had decoyed him back to his flat and held him there forcibly whilst threatening him with rape. I cannot remember the significant detail of whether or not Avelli escaped with his virtue intact, but I have been expecting ever since to find the scene reproduced in one of Mario's novels!

On our way home from Barcelona we were held up for four hours at the airport by a baggage handlers' strike. We consoled ourselves by sitting round drinking Josephine's duty free whisky out of the cap of the bottle.

11

To KEVIN FITZGERALD   *Bled, Slovenia*
Crossways, Chinnor, Oxon   *May, 1979*

Dear Kevin,
If you were here you would be longing to climb Triglaf, the highest
mountain in Slovenia (2,684 metres) and their national symbol. I view
it every morning from a safe distance. The swimming pool on the top
floor of the Hotel Park has a glass roof, so one can plunge in and
swim for the triple peak. Bled is an enchanting place and very peaceful.
The walk round the lake takes about an hour and makes a very
pleasant constitutional. Love, Elizabeth

In May 1979 the International Writers' Meeting which Slovene PEN
and The Slovene Writers' Association jointly host every year and
which used to serve also as a meeting point for the four Yugoslav
PEN Centres, was swelled by the members of two sub-committees:
Programme and Translations (set up in Stockholm) and Development
(working on revising the Rules). For those lucky enough to have been
chosen to represent their Centres on either of these committees this
was a great treat because the site of the meeting was Bled, nestling
on a little lake surrounded by green meadows and set in the heart of
the Julian Alps north-west of Ljubljana. With its little castle perched
on a high cliff overlooking the lake, its church on an island, and the
majestic triple peak of Triglaf on the skyline, Bled is like the setting
for a fairy story and it's easy to see why Tito chose it for his country
retreat and why the Slovenes now hold their meetings there rather
than on the Istrian Peninsula, at Portoroz, where I had gone as part
of David's entourage in 1971.

The hostess of all the Bled meetings was Mira Mihelic, whose great
warmth and charm I had come to know at many International PEN
meetings. By then she had been long and happily married to the artist,
France Mihelic, but her first marriage – when she was a young girl –
had taken place in the church on the island in Lake Bled, and I like to
envisage that. It must have been a very picturesque occasion, although
getting all the wedding party into boats and then up the precipitous

flight of steps to the church must have presented some problems.

It is there that the Welcome Party for the Bled meetings is usually held, but in 1979 it was in the Park Hotel, where we were all staying and where the committee meetings were also held. The English PEN representative on the Programme and Translations Committee was the novelist and man of mystery, Charles Humana, who made a rather dramatic late entrance to the first meeting of the Committee because, characteristically, he had elected to travel the cheapest possible way, overland, and had for some reason got held up at the frontier. With his black beard and aquiline nose Charles looked like a cross between a Levantine pirate and a reincarnation of Dickens, and I was amused to notice that his appearance immediately aroused the interest of Leda Mileva, who was representing Bulgarian PEN on the Committee. Because the meeting was in full swing when he arrived, there was no opportunity for introductions but when, afterwards, I went down to the room where the Welcome Party was being held, I found Leda, very uncharacteristically, hesitating on the threshold like a young girl at her first dance. When I asked her whether she would like me to introduce her to Charles, she blushingly assented. As far as I know nothing more than a mild flirtation followed, if that. I suspect that Leda found that Charles' exotic appearance was largely window-dressing.

A more fruitful encounter was that between Peter and the elderly and distinguished Chinese novelist, Yeh Chun-chan, who had frequented London literary society in the 'thirties. Mr. Yeh had been invited to Bled by the energetic Secretary of Slovene PEN, Bogdan Pogacnik, who, as well as being a journalist, also managed a male voice choir. On a recent tour of The People's Republic with this choir Bogdan had met Mr. Yeh, found that he was interested in knowing more about PEN, and invited him to Bled. This was the beginning of the delicate negotiations which led, in 1980 and 1981, to the historic step of the establishment of three PEN Centres in The People's Republic in addition to the long-standing Centre in Taipei. Because of its leisured and peaceful atmosphere Bled is a good place for such discussions.

*

To KEVIN FITZGERALD   *Rio*
Crossways, Chinnor, Oxon   *July 1979*

Dear Kevin,
I'm glad to have rolled down to Rio some day before I died. Peter of course has been here before when he ran away from school to be a

bell-hop on an American liner cruising along this coast. Some of us took the funicular up to the giant Christ statue which looms over the harbour. The view from the top was spectacular, but we nearly froze to death queuing up to get down again. Love, Elizabeth

---

The Rio Congress hotel, where we stayed and all the meetings were held, was the Gloria, in the centre of town. There we led a protected life, but were warned of the dangers of street crime if we ventured forth on our own. On the first day Peter and I were taken to lunch at a restaurant on the beach in the fashionable suburb of Copacabana and were dismayed to find children skirmishing round our table, begging for bread, and being driven off by the waiter as if they were starving dogs.

We were also very aware of the *favelas*, the shanty towns, with their ramshackle huts and lack of piped water, which were clearly visible on the slopes of the mountain.

Our Congress host was the prime mover and principal organiser of the Congress, the irrepressible Antonio Olinto, who, always accompanied by his wife, the playwright Zora Seljan, had long been a frequenter of International PEN meetings. Peter had been naturally sceptical when Antonio, at their first encounter, had presented him with one of his novels and unblushingly informed him that he (Antonio) was a great novelist To Peter's surprise he found, on reading *The Water House*, a saga of the slave trade between Brazil and West Africa, that Antonio's self-promotion had been justified.

The organisation of this Congress required all Antonio's bounce and self-confidence because, since Brazilian PEN had issued the invitation, their country had suffered such catastrophic inflation that the Congress budget had had to be slashed. Brazilian PEN bravely went ahead with the social programme they had planned, but at the reception at the fashionable Jockey Club it was Coca Cola which was served to us in paper cups which tantalisingly advertised a brand of Scotch.

On another evening the Mayor of Rio invited us to a party in the Town Hall. We hopefully assumed that this event would be taking place in the centre of Rio. Instead we had to sit in our buses for hours in the rush-hour traffic before eventually arriving, hungry and thirsty, at what looked like a giant aircraft hangar and about as welcoming. Instead of immediately being revived with food and drink, we then had to sit through a tourist promotion film showing bathing beauties on the beaches of Rio, "bums and tits", as one disgruntled delegate described it. By the time that was over, we had lost all our inhibitions and anyone who has seen PEN delegates in action when food and drink are in question can envisage the scene that followed. As each waiter came through the swing door from the kitchens with a loaded tray he was set upon and his tray stripped of all it carried. Hovering diffidently on the edge of the crowd, I was only saved from thirst and starvation by Pavel Tigrid, who somehow managed to divert a tray of food and drink in my direction. But eventually everyone did have enough to eat and drink and the mood changed. The French delegation even started dancing to the piped music.

Ironically, had it not been for Peter, Pavel would not have been present at the Congress. I think the French government had suddenly required Brazilian citizens to have visas to enter France, so Brazil had retaliated with a similar measure. Since this had only recently come into force, it had caught Pavel unawares so that he arrived without a visa and was in imminent danger of being deported back to France. It was only strong pressure by Peter on Brazilian PEN and by them on the immigration authorities that averted what would have been a very unpleasant incident.

There were plenty of other excitements to come in the meeting of the International Executive Committee because this was the year of a presidential election. Mario had been President for three years and was taking the chair for the last time. The two candidates to succeed him were Per Wästberg and Talat Halman, the Turkish poet and former Turkish Minister of Culture, now a prominent member of American PEN.

Like the practised politician he was, Talat had canvassed the Centres for their support. Per, on the other hand, had relied on his record of more than ten years in office in Swedish PEN He was elected by 36 votes to 13, which seemed to most of us a happy result, particularly considering that he had been defeated in his first bid to become President, in Ohrid five years previously. Talat swallowed his chagrin at a turn of events he had certainly not expected and beat a graceful retreat.

The other outstanding event of the Rio Congress, the culmination of the four years' work of the Development Committee, was the adoption, after many drafts and much nit-picking, of the new International PEN Rules. Henceforward the International Executive Committee was transmogrified into the Assembly of Delegates. In all other respects International PEN continued to be organised much as before.

Outside the serious business of the Congress, there were some lighter moments. I remember one evening the English delegation, forgathered in Francis King's room for some late-night refreshment, got mildly hysterical at overhearing Francis' end of a telephone conversation with room service. He was trying to order a sandwich and kept reiterating irritably "I'm *not* Mr. Gloria. I'm Mr. King", whilst it was evident to the rest of us that room service were trying to tempt him to order the hotel's own special sandwich the "Gloria Mista".

On another occasion Francis and another member of English PEN, the judge and military historian Tony Babington, walking back to the hotel at night through the public gardens, were taken short and nearly surprised by a mounted police patrol as they relieved themselves behind some bushes. They envisaged the headlines: "English novelist and judge had up for indecent exposure in Rio park".

I too nearly got into trouble. As usual, the Executive Committee had adopted a great number of resolutions which required telegrams to be sent to Heads of State all over the world calling for the release or improved treatment of the writers languishing in their gaols. I generally sent these out from International Headquarters when I returned to London, but on this occasion, because I was going to stay on in Brazil for a holiday after the Congress, I thought I would be super-efficient and send them off from the Hotel Gloria before I left Rio. This was nearly a disastrous decision. I had, as I thought, calculated roughly what the cost of sending them would be, but must have omitted a significant nought, so that the hotel presented me with a shattering bill for about £900. Peter saved me from being imprisoned for debt by calling into play the same appeal to higher authority and threat of bad publicity for Brazil that he had used to save Pavel from deportation.

Greatly relieved, I joined the party setting off the next day northwards on an internal flight to Salvador, capital of the province of Bahia, where we had arranged to spend a few days' holiday. Since Francis had had to go on to Argentina on a British Council lecture tour and so could not come with us, there were six of us in all: Josephine, Tony Babington, David and Susan Fletcher, Peter and myself. David Fletcher, then Editor of Blackwoods, had represented Scottish PEN in Rio. Salvador was the place where the slave ships from West Africa used to land their cargoes and, as a result of miscegenation, a majority of the population of the city are a very handsome coffee colour. The city is constructed on two levels, with a lift to take pedestrians from the harbour to the upper, central part of the town. This makes it a complicated place to drive in, but this did not daunt Peter, who drove the minivan we hired for a day to explore the interior. The problem of getting out of the city was exacerbated by his preference for not consulting maps but driving by guess and by god. Susan Fletcher, who was a teacher and an organised person, did not understand this foible of Peter's and tried to direct him, whilst the rest of us kept quiet and hoped for the best. In the end, whether because of or in spite of Susan's directions, we did find our way out of Salvador and drove into the interior until we found ourselves in a run-down, almost deserted settlement which bore some resemblance to a frontier town in a Western film. By this time we were hungry for lunch and went into the only restaurant we could find. The food they produced was not very appetising and I was in any case put off it by what appeared to be urine on the floor in the corner of the room. Fortunately Susan, who we felt might have refused to eat there, was sitting with her back to the offending corner, and, although the rest of us noticed it, we were too hungry to risk a comment.

On another day we decided to go in the opposite direction and visit one of the off-shore islands. Owing to a misunderstanding we got on the wrong boat and landed on a much less inhabited island than the one we had been aiming for. In fact where we landed there was no sign of any habitation at all. Luckily for us the only other passenger on our boat, a small dark man in a beautiful embroidered shirt, fell into conversation with Peter and introduced himself as Mr. Julius. Since Peter happened to be sitting apart from the rest of us and since he was the only one amongst us with any Latin American language (he had acquired Spanish in his Barcelona prison and improved it when he was running a hotel in Mexico) Mr. Julius jumped to the conclusion that he was our guide. He addressed Peter familiarly as "Stob", perhaps assuming that his name was El Stob, and said he could offer a good deal to our party if we would put ourselves in his care. This seemed like a good way out of the difficulty of arriving on an apparently uninhabited island, and Peter accepted on our behalf. It turned out to be an excellent move. When we landed Mr. Julius produced from somewhere nearby a battered car, in which he drove us to the other side of the island, where there was a beautiful beach. When we had swum in the warm sea, we ate our lunch al fresco, having been encouraged to go behind a screen and make our choice from various delicious stews cooked in oil drums set over wood fires and stirred by large black ladies. Replete, we lay blissfully in the shade until Mr. Julius told us it was time for him to drive us to the other end of the island to connect with the boat back to the mainland. It was fortunate that the boat's timetable was a very relaxed Brazilian one because, not surprisingly considering the state of Mr. Julius' car and of the island roads, we had a blow-out en route. We were worried about missing the boat, but he simply roared with laughter at this mishap and, sure enough, when he had changed the wheel and driven us to the harbour we still had time to spare.

In memory of that happy day on the island Josephine and I still call Peter "Stob" when we want to distinguish him from another Peter active in PEN, Peter Day, the publisher.

12

1979 was rounded off for Peter and me by visits to Brussels and Budapest which were not connected with any International PEN event. Carlos de Radzitzky had managed to get us invited to a very grand reception at the Hotel de Ville to celebrate the thousandth anniversary of the founding of Brussels. He and his elegant wife Gigi also entertained us in their small house in the Rue de Fond'Roy. It was a pleasure to see Carlos at home, where the space seemed to be almost entirely taken up with his books and jazz records. Gigi, although she had her own career as a teacher, seemed chiefly dedicated to keeping Carlos happy, which she did to perfection.

Since we were so close to the field of Waterloo and I had never seen it, Peter hired a car and drove me out there. We climbed to the summit of the *Lion de Waterloo*, the gigantic earth mound erected by the Dutch on the spot where William of Orange was wounded, which gave us a commanding view of the battlefield and enabled Peter, as a military historian, to explain Wellington's and Blucher's tactics to me.

From Brussels we went on to Budapest, where we had been invited as the guests of Hungarian PEN. Laszlo Kéry, who had conveyed the invitation, had asked Peter if he would address a meeting of the members and, so that I should not feel left out, had said that they would be very pleased if I too would speak for about ten minutes. This threw me into a considerable panic. Josephine, seeing my alarm, kindly lent me a book on public speaking, from which I gathered that one should never read a speech, but should merely make a few notes and speak from them. I thought I should feel safer if I had written a speech, so I did, and then compromised by learning it by heart and throwing away the typescript. At about this time, when I was down in Sussex visiting my parents, I was invited out to a dinner party by people I scarcely knew and, in a misguided attempt to entertain the company, told them that I had been practising my speech in front of the bathroom mirror, but could not manage to stretch it beyond five minutes. My host cast a sardonic look at me and said: "That's because you're speaking too fast. Personally I can scarcely understand a word you say. All you need do is deliver your speech at half the speed." When I repeated this remark to Josephine, she was indignant on my behalf and asked: "Who was this man?" When I replied that he was a retired anaesthetist, she at once produced the theory that his mental powers had been slowed down as a result of inhaling too much of the anaesthetic which he was administering to his patients.

In the event the meeting of Hungarian PEN was very friendly and unalarming. The members sat round small tables, as if in a literary café and, since Peter allowed me to speak first, my ordeal was soon over. Lászlo sat between us and made consecutive translations of both our speeches. I thought mine sounded very impressive in Hungarian.

We were given a warm welcome in Budapest and had the privilege of being invited to the houses of both their grand old men, Gyulá Illyés and István Vás. They and their wives entertained us most hospitably. They formed an interesting contrast: Illyés, then in his late seventies, thick-set and with a strong face that looked as if it had been carved from a rock, might have been a model for a peasant in a Brueghel painting, and his wife was in the same mold. Vás, a few years younger, had more fine-drawn features and a more cosmopolitan air. He and his artist wife, Petra, both spoke good English, so we did not have to communicate with them through an interpreter.

We were also granted an interview with the Minister of Culture, who was surprisingly young and quite attractive. Iván Boldizsár and Lászlo Kéry both accompanied us to this and Iván had a private interview with the Minister whilst we waited in the anteroom. Lászlo remarked drily that Iván was no doubt telling the Minister what to say to us. At this distance of time I can't remember what he did say. I am sure that Peter's role in the conversation was to stress the active part that the Hungarian Centre played in the affairs of International PEN and their importance to us. It was, after all, the chief purpose of our visit to make this point to the government and to get good coverage in the local press for Hungarian PEN. Having done our duty, we were put in the charge of a charming couple, both of whom were writers and PEN members, who drove us the thirty or forty miles north of Budapest to the Bend in the River Danube. This is where the great river is halted by the Budapest Mountains in the easterly course which it has been pursuing since leaving Vienna and turns south towards Budapest. On its way it passes the picturesque town of Szentendre, which has a thriving artists' colony. We wandered round in the sunshine admiring the red and blue houses built by the Serbs and Greeks who first settled the town in the Middle Ages when they were fleeing the Turks. In all this area one is very aware of being at the centre of the ebb and flow of many peoples over the centuries.

On our return to Budapest we were entertained to drinks by the British Cultural Attaché and then taken on to dinner in a very attractive old restaurant, up on the hill, in Buda. By the time we arrived at the restaurant I needed to go to the ladies' room, but, not wanting to get separated from the rest of the party, I decided to wait until we had been seated and had ordered our meal and then excuse myself. I carried out this programme and set out, as I thought, back to where we had come in and left our coats. I had not reckoned with the confusing layout of the restaurant, which was made up of a series of interconnecting rooms, and instead of finding the cloakroom, I found myself back at our table. Mimi Kéry, who was seated opposite me, asked me whether there was anything wrong and when I explained my dilemma, sprang up to guide me. Unfortunately it turned out that her sense of direction was even worse than mine and we twice ended up by the entrance to the kitchen instead of at the cloakroom. Eventually we found what we were looking for and I was able to relieve myself. By this time, however, the whole restaurant were following our progress with interest and, not realising that we had finally succeeded in our quest, kept helpfully directing us back to the cloakroom when we were trying to return to our table. By the time I resumed my seat next to the Second Secretary at the British Embassy I was much more embarrassed than if I had had to make another speech. On their annual visits to London on their way to Stratford to satisfy László's enthusiasm for Shakespeare the Kérys often took me out to lunch and I used to point out to Mimi that the layout of restaurants in London was far simpler and less hazardous than in Budapest.

13

*We're back here again, this time for a big International Conference
and – unexpectedly – a brush with history. Tito died in hospital in
Ljubljana just after our plane touched down there. This is obviously
a cataclysmic event for all Yugoslavia and people are frightened of a
Russian invasion. Our Slovene hosts are keeping their cool and doing
their best to carry on with the Conference without appearing disre-
spectful to the President's memory. Love, Elizabeth.*

The party from London bound for the Bled Conference consisted of
the two English PEN delegates: Josephine and the novelist Catherine
Dupre, Francis (a guest of honour), Charles Humana (for the Programme and Translations Committee), Peter and Barbara Elstob and
myself. We were booked to stay the night in Ljubljana so that we
could travel up to Bled the next morning. As we gathered in the rather
gloomy bar of the hotel before dinner that evening the dire news of
President Tito's death was whispered from one group to another of
our fellow guests and eventually reached us. A week's national mourn-
ing was declared and some delegates on their way to attend our Conference were turned back at the frontier. Feeling that we were present
at a moment in history, some of us went out early the next morning
to watch Tito's body being transported to the railway station on its
way to Belgrade for the state funeral. It was pouring with rain but
the streets were lined with people who stood in dead silence to watch
the coffin pass.

Because of the crowds our little group got split up and I found
myself walking with the Polish delegate, Artur Miedzyrzecki, whom
I had not met before. With his white hair, slightly protuberant brown
eyes and almost childlike smile, he was an appealing figure, with
whom I immediately felt at ease. It was only when I got to know him
better on several visits to Poland that I realised that as well as being
a very distinguished writer, he had shown great courage throughout
his life, both when fighting in the Second World War and in his

resistance to the communist regime. French was his preferred second language, but he was also very fluent in English, and a great talker in any language. Since he spoke rather softly and it was difficult to keep abreast of each other on the narrow pavement, I missed quite a lot of his conversation, but it did not seem to matter as he burbled on quite happily without waiting for my reply. This was the beginning of a close friendship, both with him and his wife, the poet Julia Hartwig.

Our Slovene hosts were now faced with the dilemma of whether or not to continue with the Conference. They solved it with their usual pragmatism. Since it was felt that it would not be fitting to have business discussions whilst the President was still lying in state, the usual order was reversed, the Assembly of Delegates being put off until the end of the meeting, when the funeral had taken place. The Conference therefore started with the literary sessions. The social programme was officially cancelled, but nevertheless when we all drifted down to the dining-room at the Hotel Park on the first evening, wine was served and we had an unofficial welcome party.

The absence of a social programme left more time for fraternising with the other delegates, either in the swimming pool or on one of the many lovely walks – round the lake or through the meadows, which in May are filled with flowers. As well as rowing boats, there are also horse-drawn carriages always waiting for hire by the landing stage at the end of the lake, and Nancy Ing and I hired one of these to take us up the steep winding road to the little castle. The English delegation also made an excursion there which had an unfortunate outcome. Catherine Dupre fell on the uneven cobbles of the castle courtyard, broke her ankle and had to be taken to hospital in Ljubljana to be put in plaster.

I walked round the lake with Alex Blokh and the Israeli poet Bathsheva Sheriff, who always attends the Bled meetings wearing the dramatic, broad-brimmed black felt hat which is her trademark. I scarcely knew her then, although I was to get to know her and her husband Mordecai very well in future years, and I was rather intimidated by the hat. Alex I only knew from a distance as the urbane Unesco representative, and I was likewise intimidated by the carnation he always wore in his buttonhole. I had been very disturbed when Peter had recently told me that he had approached Alex to see if he would be interested, since his retirement from Unesco was imminent, in taking on the job of International Secretary. From the beginning Peter had made no secret of the fact that he wanted to be free to return to his own writing as soon as he managed to find a suitable successor, but I had, ostrich-like, tried to blot out this possibility from my mind.

After six years of happy (if sometimes long-distance) collaboration, I could not envisage working with anyone but Peter, and certainly not with an alarmingly elegant and sophisticated Frenchman who had been a Unesco functionary. Alex had by this time expressed interest in standing for election and, since Peter had impressed upon him that I came with the job, we were in the process of sizing each other up. Bled provided just the right surroundings for getting to know each other, and I discovered that there was a very warm and attractive personality hidden behind the polished façade. I believe it was our shared pleasure in watching the antics of the ducks on the lake that first persuaded me that it would be possible for us to work together.

*

It was at the Bled meeting of the Assembly of Delegates that Michael Scammell announced that he had recently resigned from his job as Editor of *Index on Censorship* in order to concentrate on his writing. This meant that he could not continue to use the facilities of the *Index* office for the work of the Writers in Prison Committee. Since International Headquarters at Dilke Street were already overcrowded he was looking for a one-room office elsewhere in London. He also mentioned the possibility that International PEN and the Writers in Prison Committee might, if finance permitted, find offices which they could share. What had happened was that Peter, hearing of Michael's intention to look for a separate office for the Writers in Prison Committee, had sensed the danger of the Committee, which was already to some extent autonomous, breaking away entirely from the control of the parent body, and had hastily taken steps to checkmate any such scheme. An additional consideration was that he was preparing the ground for his successor as International Secretary, who he felt could not be expected to share the small back office at Dilke Street with Josephine. This was how it came about in April of the following year that Peter, Bill Barazetti and I, taking the International PEN files with us, upped sticks and moved to King Street, Covent Garden, completing the split with English PEN which had begun when Josephine succeeded Peter as Secretary.

Before that, however, there was an International Conference in Copenhagen in February and, since there was an unusually long gap between that and the Bled meeting, Peter and I had time to pay a visit to the Austrian and Polish Centres. This took place in October when the Vienna Woods were in their full autumn colouring. Peter came on to Vienna from the Unesco General Conference in Belgrade, so I travelled separately, direct from London, and met him at the hotel. As usual, we were made very warmly welcome by our hosts. We were conscientiously looked after by Peter von Tramin, whom we knew well as the Austrian delegate at many international meetings. Tall and thin, with a drooping cigarette holder, he seemed the epitome of an effete aristocrat – he was indeed a Baron, although we were told that those were two a penny in Austria – but he confided in us that he had a passion for riding, which he mostly did across the frontier on the plains of Hungary. He was a difficult man to warm to, but it was a great shock when we heard the following year that he had committed suicide. There was no sign of this tragedy to come when, with his attractive blonde girl friend, he took us out to dinner in Vienna. He also escorted us on a visit to the PEN Branch in Burgenland, a rural province to the south-east of the capital, where we were entertained to lunch in a small country house, set in its own park.

From Vienna we took the night train through Czechoslovakia to Warsaw (a journey I was to make again, with Francis and Peter Day, after the Vienna Congress of 1991). Although this was only the first of many visits to Poland for me, it was the most exciting because it was the year when Solidarity had come into being and there was a heady feeling of optimism in the air. We were immediately given Solidarnosc badges to wear. Polish PEN had an additional reason for pleasure: Czeslaw Milosz had just been awarded the Nobel Prize for Literature. My most striking memory of our stay in Warsaw is of being taken to see a film (from the German archive presumably) of the destruction of Warsaw, and then emerging, blinking into the sunshine of the cobbled Old Town Square, which we had just seen flattened and which was now miraculously restored in every detail. Aside from that I remember chiefly the people we met and who welcomed us with such warmth. There was dear Artur, of course, and his wife Julia, who gave him such loving support that her own fame as a poet might easily be overlooked. There was also the President of Polish PEN, Juliusz Zulawski, with his craggily handsome face. And there was Wladyslaw Bartoszewski, an unforgettable figure, then Secretary of Polish PEN, later to become Polish Ambassador in Vienna. He looked like a benevolent raven and spoke with the speed and delivery of a machine gun, so that we were not at all surprised to learn that he had worn out relays of interrogators – both Nazi and Communist – in his various periods of imprisonment. Since he spoke neither English nor French, Peter and I could only communicate with him through an interpreter, but the force of his personality as well as his great charm came through undiminished.

In Krakow, the old capital, we were looked after by the President of the PEN Branch. He was a very distinguished and handsome man, an art historian, who wore well-cut tweeds and spoke absolutely perfect English. He seemed like a throwback to an earlier generation when the aristocracy of Europe were closely related. Indeed when we were being shown round one of the picture galleries, my attention was caught by a portrait of a nobleman of an earlier century who closely resembled him and who I was later told was one of his family.

It was from him that I first heard the story behind the interrupted trumpet call which is sounded from the higher of the two towers of the Church of St. Mary Of The Assumption in the magnificent Market Square. The legend is that a watchman on the tower, sounding the alarm at the approach of the invading Tartars, was shot through the throat by an arrow before he could finish, so for the past seven hundred years the trumpet call with its broken off ending has been sounded every hour. The trumpeter now keeps watch for fires rather than Tartars. According to our guide, the only time when the call was not sounded (unfortunately when a visiting dignitary had been brought to the square specially to hear it) was when the fireman had been imbibing and was too drunk to make it.

14

To Kevin FitzGerald   *Copenhagen*
Crossways, Chinnor, Oxon   *February 1981*

Dear Kevin,
Copenhagen is under snow and looking very picturesque. Our hotel,
the Admiral, ia a beautiful converted warehouse down by the docks
where the ferries to and from Sweden come and go. This is a small
meeting, which is really more fun than a Congress since you can really
get to know people. Much love, Elizabeth

Gavin Ewart, invited to participate in the Poetry Seminar which we
organised in Copenhagen in conjunction with Unesco, wrote a "Words-
worthian self-apostrophe" as he lay in bed in the Hotel Admiral and
watched the snow drift down outside his fourth-floor window:

> *"Relax. Relax. It's 8 o'clock. The gulls patrol the harbour.*
> *It's a perfect Danish winter morning.*
> *A man is fooling about with a snow-machine,*
> *A brush that whirrs a pathway on the quay.*
> *A little snow-blizzard looks to be blowing,*
> *But you're inside and warm; with loved ones far away . . ."*

Because it was a small meeting it had a friendly informality which
the larger Congresses cannot achieve. It was also typically Danish.
Instead of a big party for everyone, all the publishers entertained us
in small groups and, Copenhagen being such a small and compact
city, we could drift from one party to another, getting merrier as we
went. At one of these parties, when we were all seated round a long
table, drinking good wine and reciting our party pieces, a disagreeable
overseas member of English PEN – a journalist living in Copenhagen
– got into dispute with one of the Canadian delegates, a sensitive
québecoise poet, and called her a stupid woman. More accustomed
to male admiration than such rudeness, she burst into tears and
rushed out of the room, but was retrieved and comforted by a male
delegate from the Centre Suisse Romande. So even that incident ended
happily The rest of us had a lovely time before we finally drifted back

to the Hotel Admiral through the snow in a very mellow state.

Since Peter had now officially announced that he would be resigning as International Secretary at the Lyons Congress in September, a Selection Committee of nine people from the most active Centres in various parts of the world was set up to choose his successor. The only candidate was Alex Blokh, so they interviewed him and agreed to put him forward for election at the Lyons Congress later that year.

When the business of the Conference was over most of the English delegation crammed into a minivan with Peter at the wheel as we set off to drive round the coast of Denmark. Our first port of call was the Louisiana Museum of Contemporary Art, a graceful nineteenth century white building set in handsome grounds about twenty miles north of Copenhagen. It apparently acquired its name from the odd fact that the owner of the house before it became a museum had three wives, all of whom were called Louise. Elsinore Castle was closed, so we had to content ourselves with gazing across the water at its formidable bulk. We drove on through the flat, snow-covered countryside until we arrived at a point on the coast from which we could look across the strait of Skagerrak towards Norway. Or was it the strait of Kattegat and Sweden we looked towards? All I can now recall is the splendid names of both straits.

Barbara Noble, the novelist and publisher, who was one of our group and less accustomed than the rest of us to adventuring with Peter, was very impressed with his dashing style of driving and said that he seemed to her the epitome of a Renaissance man, which pleased him. On our way back to Copenhagen we visited the home of Erik Vagn Jensen, the Secretary of Danish PEN, who looked more like a bluff sea captain than a writer. According to Scandinavian custom, we had to take off our shoes in the front hall and choose from an assortment of slippers, a sensible arrangement in a snowy winter.

*

The move from Dilke Street to Covent Garden in April 1981 was not as traumatic as the move from Glebe House to Dilke Street had been. English PEN kindly continued to give house room to the box files of Congress records which had nearly crushed me on our previous move, so there were only a few filing cabinets and desks to shift. The problem was how to fit the staff, few of us though there were, into our two tiny offices on the first floor front of the Africa Centre at 38 King Street. The smaller, inner, office, a mere slit which could just accommodate two desks, was shared by Peter and Michael Scammell, boxing and coxing, with the second desk for Kathleen. The outer office, alongside it, was large enough to accommodate three desks – just. The one with its back to the window was reserved for Bill, who came to King Street to do the International PEN accounts on Tuesdays. The other two were shared between my new part-time assistant, Diana Whitaker, Patricia Markowsky Nahaylo, the Canadian girl (of Ukrainian extraction) who had joined the staff of the Writers in Prison Committee and me. I was in King Street every day except Wednesday, when I still worked at Dilke Street, taking the Minutes for their Executive Committee meetings and letting in members for the evening meetings. This complicated patchwork and lack of space required tolerance from all of us, particularly when, on one disastrous occasion, I tripped over the flex of the Writers in Prison Committee computer, unplugging it and so causing them to lose their carefully compiled list of prisoners. Diana was a very welcome addition to our number since she was not only good-looking, with a charming telephone manner, but also spoke excellent French – all of which qualities particularly endeared her to Alex when he came amongst us. The reason for our good fortune in finding someone of her calibre was her ill fortune; she was then in her thirties and had for some years been suffering from multiple sclerosis. This had not noticeably affected her, except that she found it difficult to walk any distance, but it did mean that she had not the stamina to take on a full-time job, so working part-time for us, in a job without too much pressure, suited her very well. We all enjoyed working in Covent Garden. We were just a stone's throw from the Piazza and could, tantalisingly, hear the music coming from it and even, by leaning out of the window, get a glimpse of whatever was going on there. For lunch-hours and for meeting friends after work there were dozens of eating places and coffee bars to choose from, not to mention the Calabash Restaurant, in the basement of our building, serving strange stews in suitably ethnic decor. The Africa Centre had a ramshackle charm of its own and it was refreshing to be surrounded by so many black faces – not often seen in PEN at that time when we had so few Centres in Africa. As Per said, when the Assembly of Delegates met in the hall at the back of the building in March 1982, the slight eccentricity of the surroundings and the rather makeshift arrangements provided an atmosphere which was far more suited to PEN than smarter and more expensive offices would have been, even if we could have afforded them. So, in spite of the problems of sharing desks and practically sitting in each other's laps, we were sad when our ten-year lease at 38 King Street expired in 1991 and we had to move to the more spacious offices, but less attractive surroundings, of Charterhouse Buildings, between Clerkenwell and the western fringe of the City. It felt like exile.

15

I see from Peter's report to the Lyons Congress the following September that after Copenhagen he and I went to Paris to attend a meeting with other Non-Governmental Organisations at Unesco Headquarters. My memory has mercifully blotted out the whole occasion except for a sensation of deep boredom and slight nausea which Unesco Headquarters always induced in me. Fortunately I did not usually accompany Peter when he went there, but this time we were combining it with attending French PEN's annual dinner, which was much more fun, and then going on to Lyons to inspect the arrangements for the Congress. The President of French PEN at that time was the novelist and poet René Tavernier (father of the film director Bertrand Tavernier) and it was because he was a native of Lyons that the Congress was to be held there. At that time he was a big, bulky man, who looked as if he had partaken too lavishly of the famous cuisine of his native city, but in his youth (when, under the Nazi occupation, he had produced an underground magazine) he had apparently been very handsome and he still had great charm and a pleasing, if somewhat elephantine, sense of humour. He drove us down to Lyons, accompanied by the lady who ran the French PEN office and would have to bear the brunt of the Congress organisation, Mauricette Berthier. She was petite and lively, with strikingly blue eyes. Being a widow without any children she evidently found PEN an outlet for her energies. Our previous contacts had been limited to telephone conversations, which were always a struggle for me because (with typical French obstinacy, as it seemed to me!) she resolutely refused either to speak or attempt to understand English. I am better at grappling with French conversation face to face than I am on the telephone, so I welcomed this chance to get to know her and brush up my French at the same time. René's English, by contrast, was so good that he enjoyed showing it off by indulging in outrageous puns.

We stayed for a couple of nights at the Hotel Ibis, on the outskirts of the city, which was going to be the cheapest of the hotels on offer to the Congress participants. It was part of a chain, a package tour hotel like the Penta (of London Congress fame). It was perfectly adequate, but rather basic, and certainly not the sort of hotel at which René was accustomed to stay. So we spent a pleasant time visiting the other Congress locations and sampling the offerings of the best restaurants in Lyons, while in the evenings we returned reluctantly to the Ibis. As it hove into sight, René would exclaim, with simulated enthusiasm: "Ah! Quel plaisir! Once more we return to the delightful Hotel Ibis." When Peter and I flew home I was fascinated to see that one of the Ibis Hotel chain was under construction at Heathrow. I immediately sent René a post card to inform him of this exciting development.

*

To Kevin FitzGerald   *Lyons*
Crossways, Chinnor, Oxon   *September 1981*

Dear Kevin,
This is not really a very enjoyable Congress. We're all dotted about in different hotels some of them miles from the Palais des Congrès so that it's almost impossible to socialise after hours. The weather has not been very good either – a terrific thunder storm when I went to meet the International Treasurer at the airport. Perhaps I'm just gloomy because this is Peter's last Congress as International Secretary. He, on the other hand, can't wait to go! Love, Elizabeth

The Lyons Congress marked PEN's Diamond Jubilee, but lacked the grandeur of scale of some Congresses (Vienna and Seoul for instance) and the intimacy of smaller meetings, such as Copenhagen. René had recently been severely mugged and turned up with two spectacular black eyes (a precedent which Norman Mailer followed, though with only one black eye, when he was host President to the New York Congress in 1986 and had had a recent bout with a prize fighter). Alex was duly elected to succeed Peter and pointed out in his eloquent speech of thanks that it was the first time that the International Secretary of PEN had not been an Englishman. Carlos then read out a resolution, submitted by the French Centre and his own Francophone Belgian Centre and supported by eighteen other Centres from all parts of the world, proposing that Peter be elected an International Vice-President in gratitude for the fact that "in his difficult office he has demonstrated unfailing competence and perfect impartiality and has carried out his duties with an integrity and a dignity from which International PEN has not ceased to benefit on every occasion". Peter was elected to great acclaim.

The most important event on the Lyons social programme was a banquet given by French PEN on the Thursday evening at the *Cuvage des Compagnons du Beaujolais* at Lacenas. This was where Peter was to be given his leaving present – a handsome cheque – and to make his farewell speech. Unfortunately Lacenas is some distance from Lyons and one of the buses broke down on the way there, so the English delegation, amongst others, arrived late and had to sit at a draughty table near the door. As far as I remember, the food was quite good, and the Beaujolais was certainly excellent and flowed freely and when we had finished eating there was music and dancing to lift our spirits. The drawback of the Cuvage was that it was a converted wine cellar, its vaulted roof supported by pillars which effectively restricted our vision so that when Per presented Peter with the cheque collected from the Centres for his leaving present, and Peter made his speech of thanks and farewell, they were both only visible and audible to a small section of the room. Everyone else went on eating and drinking obliviously.

The Congress concluded in Paris, and French PEN very bravely arranged that we should all be transported there by the new fast train, the TGV, on its trial run. There was a certain amount of chaos on the station platform as we all tried to heave our luggage aboard the train, which was much higher than the platform. (The train was late so all the porters had gone to lunch.) Francis, with his usual good manners, offered to help Sybille Bedford with her luggage and then found himself cast in the role of conveyor belt for other ladies' baggage. He commented afterwards that Sybille had thanked him profusely and shown her gratitude by buying him a drink, whereas some of the other ladies had taken his services for granted. I observed that Nadine Gordimer, by contrast, who was a guest of honour at the Congress, had her suitcase on wheels and was quite self-sufficient.

Once on the train we were served with luncheon trays as we watched the French countryside speed by us. I remember it as a smooth ride, but Per tells me that this was not so. Apparently the wine waiter succeeded in pouring red wine all over the Duchesse de la Rochefoucauld, in spite of her screams of protest, and Per, in his seat across the corridor, got splashed with a few drops, as if of blood.

The Closing Ceremony took place at the Sorbonne, where, as Francis reported, with exquisite tact, in the English Centre *Broadsheet*, there were "a number of those orations which the French deliver with so much eloquence and panache. On a quieter, more reflective note, Per Wästberg also spoke." According to my programme there were ten speakers, including the Minister of Culture, Jack Lang, and the Director-General of Unesco, Amadou Mahtar M'Bow. It certainly seemed a wearily long time before we were released and transported to the Hotel de Ville, where we were received by the Mayor, Jacques Chirac. His official hostess on that occasion was his Deputy, Monique Garnier-Lançon, later to become Secretary of French PEN

After the reception the various delegations all went their separate ways. Some of the English party, joined by Catherine Dupre and Charlotte Hough, who had not been at the Congress, had booked for the weekend at different hotels in the Place St. Sulpice, Rue Bonaparte area. On the Saturday morning we forgathered for an outing, but were so stupified with post-Congress exhaustion that we spent a considerable time wandering round like a herd of sheep without a shepherd and losing our way on the Metro until we finally ended up at the Gare de Lyons for a late lunch before catching the train to Versailles. I think Catherine and Charlotte found us very boring company because we were still in Congress mode and full of gossip about who had said what to whom and when.

Back in London I had to come to grips with reality once more and accomplish the switch to a new International Secretary. Technically Peter was supposed to be working in double harness with Alex until the end of 1981, but in fact he had been invited to represent International PEN at an Asian Writers' Conference in The Philippines in December, so he handed over his duties to Alex almost immediately after his return from France to London and I think it was in October that he and Barbara set off for the Far East. Certainly it was a letter from him with a Manila postmark that I stuffed into my pocket as I left for Heathrow on a chilly November morning to fly to Charles de Gaulle for my first working session with Alex.

Alex and Nadia had long since moved from the Rue des Orchidées, where Liz Warner used to ring them up to set up dinner invitations for David. They now lived (as they still do) in an elegant house on Square Montsouris, a steep, cobbled street on the edge of Parc Montsouris, on the south-eastern fringe of Paris. Alex had booked me a room in a nearby hotel and it was there, shivering in the rather cold and comfortless surroundings, that I reread Peter's letter before changing to go out to dinner with the Blokhs. The letter, coming as it did from so far away, brought home to me the change in my circumstances. Both PEN and I had reached a watershed in our lives and I felt I had temporarily lost the will to cross it. The sunny day in August thirteen years before when David had interviewed me at Glebe House seemed like a lost world. Then I remembered that the other guest at dinner that night was to be Lawrence Durrell, who was an old friend of the Blokhs. I thought wryly how pleased David would have been to dine in such company. With this inspiriting thought, I put Peter's letter aside and went out to 34 Square Montsouris for dinner.

Part III

ALEXANDRE BLOKH

*The Man with the
Carnation in his Buttonhole*

1

To sweeten the pill of no longer having an International Secretary
resident in London Alex had thought up a scheme by which he and
I would alternate visits to each other. One month he would come to
London; the next I would go to Paris. This sounded delightful in
theory, but quickly proved impractical. Apart from Alex's small study,
the Blokhs' tall thin house in Square Montsouris had nowhere I could
work, and, although Nadia was kind to me and, having taken stock
of the limitations of my wardrobe, even generously offered to introduce me to the shop where she bought her elegant designer outfits,
she clearly would not welcome my frequent presence crouched over
a portable typewriter at her dining table. In any case Alex spent the
greater part of every day keeping up his contacts at Unesco or
attending meetings at the Société des Gens de Lettres. The result was
that I did a phenomenal amount of sightseeing and became better
acquainted with Paris, but felt that I was wasting PEN's time and
money. When I put this to Alex I think he was greatly relieved. He
had not wanted to go back on his word and deprive me of a perk,
but, as a dedicated anglophile, loved coming to London and particularly the London theatres. Before his monthly visit I was always
requested to buy theatre tickets, if possible Shakespeare, for which he
had a passion. Sometimes Nadia, who also loved coming to London,
would accompany him. At first they stayed at a small hotel in Blooms-

bury, then joined the Sloane Club, to which Lavinia introduced them. From the Sloane Club they graduated to the Special Forces Club, in Hans Crescent, for which Alex qualified by virtue of his wartime membership of the Resistance. If he came to London on his own he would arrive at lunchtime one day and depart on the afternoon of the next. In that short time he would manage to fit in a theatre and a visit to a gallery – pictures being another passion of his – as well as transferring the toppling contents of his in tray onto my desk, dictating, at a speed too great for my rusty shorthand, replies which were sometimes in such convoluted English that I had to rephrase them in any case. He always accepted with a very good grace the revised versions which I presented to him for his signature. Replies in French he wrote out by hand, which presented another problem because his handwriting was almost totally illegible. Fortunately my assistant Diana's French was much better than mine, so I was able to leave to her the task of decoding them.

Alex's zest for London life and enjoyment of the idiosyncrasies of PEN were infectious, and he adapted gracefully to the shortage of space and staff in our offices at the Africa Centre. I had been a little apprehensive about his reactions to having to play box and cox with Michael Scammell at the director's desk (once David's) which took up most of the space at the window end of the smaller of our two small offices, and having to make do with only two members of staff, and those both part-time (I was still working for English PEN on Wednesdays). I was reassured when, on one of his earliest visits, seeing what was the most immediate job that needed doing, he took off his jacket (a carnation in the buttonhole, as always) and got down to helping Diana and me collate some documents which had to be sent out to the Centres.

The Yugoslav Centres had jointly invited us to hold the 1982 Congress in Belgrade, but had had to cancel it at short notice because of economic restrictions imposed by their government, so we were left without a Congress in Alex's first year. Since it was important that we at least have a meeting of the Assembly of Delegates as soon as possible, we held one in March in the elegant, but long and narrow, hall in the Africa Centre. It was convenient to have the meeting in the same building as our offices, but in other ways it was a nightmare to organise and the delegates – particularly René Tavernier – grumbled loudly at what Per at a later meeting aptly described as the "disordered intimacy" of the Africa Centre. We did provide them with chairs, but there was no room for tables. We could not afford simultaneous interpretation, even if there had been room for interpreters' booths, so consecutive interpretation between English and French where necessary had to be provided by Alex. We had hired microphones and amplifying equipment, but, since the Africa Centre was notoriously subject to theft, we dared not leave anything removable in the hall when the Assembly was not in session. This meant hefting it all up the steep and narrow spiral staircase to our first-floor offices, so at the end of the first day I looked round for a sufficiently lusty male delegate whom I could enlist to do this job. I thought I had found the ideal candidate in the red-bearded Secretary of Irish PEN, Arthur Flynn, but my confidence was misplaced. Arthur did indeed express charming willingness to help, but then, in some remarkable way, managed to dematerialise and not be seen again until the next morning. So, muttering darkly, I had to do the job myself.

Since there was no host Centre for this meeting, delegates had to make their own hotel arrangements. We did, however, manage to lay on two parties. English PEN gave one in the Studio at Dilke Street for the visiting delegates, and Tony Babington, as a Master of the Middle Temple, kindly arranged for us to have a reception in their beautiful Hall. The Assembly had just, at the urging of the Dutch, elected a Friesian Centre, and I remember their delegates, superannuated hippies, dressed in jeans and with long hair tied back in pony tails, looking incongruous in those formal surroundings. I am afraid they may have got the impression that PEN was too bourgeois to suit them. At any rate they were never seen or heard of again.

No Assembly is complete without a row, and the most notable one at this meeting was when Francis, reporting on the progress of the PEN/UNESCO Short Story Anthology of which he was Editor, remarked in passing that because the stories chosen had to be passed as representative by the National Commissions of the countries from which they came, no stories by exiled writers could be included. Shock, horror! It had clearly never occurred to most of the delegates that this was bound to be a condition of any anthology produced with Unesco money. Alex saw himself possibly faced, at this early stage of his secretaryship, with the unpalatable task of going to Unesco and saying that PEN wanted to cancel its contract. He offered to raise money elsewhere for a separate anthology of the work of exiled writers, but this did not placate the fierce opposition of a group led by Margareta Ekström and Mario Vargas Llosa, who said that such censorship by Unesco was absolutely against the ideals of PEN. The discussion became very heated and Per, from the Chair, diplomatically proposed that a final decision on this item be adjourned until the following morning. Here Fate intervened. The next day was a Sunday and Mario, the most ardent opponent of proceeding with the anthology, did not realise that Covent Garden underground station was shut on Sundays.

He was carried on to Holborn and so arrived at the meeting, after it had accepted Per's suggestion that the present anthology should be proceeded with, but should include in its preface a declaration that PEN would not in future accept this kind of censorship.

The Centres were united in their concern for their colleagues in Poland, and this was the first of many meetings at which the Polish situation was discussed. The optimism which Peter and I had found when we visited that country in 1980, at the birth of Solidarity, had been extinguished by General Jaruzelski's declaration of martial law the following year, and many of the writers we had met then were now interned. Antonia Fraser, as Chair of English PEN's Writers in Prison Committee, reported on the demonstration which we had held outside the Polish embassy in Portland Place, holding up a banner emblazoned with the legend "Free Polish Writers Now". A letter of protest had been handed in and Harold Pinter had made a speech. This had all been meticulously organised by Josephine, in close cooperation with the police, and was the model of many future demonstrations outside embassies: Turkish, Malawian, Iranian, Nigerian . . ., the banner being altered to suit the occasion. The aim was always to assemble as many members as possible to provide solid back-up to a few notabilities, such as the Pinters, who would attract the attention of the Press. There was usually no reaction from within the beleaguered embassy and it was difficult to know whether anything had been achieved, but in this case we did hear later that our Polish friends had been much cheered in their internment to hear Harold Pinter's speech via the World Service of the BBC.

2

Dear Kevin,
Josephine and I have borrowed the Blokhs' house for two weeks
on this beautiful, untouristy island. Athens was scorching, but here
there is a bit of breeze off the sea and we eat our meals on a vine-
shaded patio, so life is very pleasant. J. is writing a book and I am
lazing about, reading. I may be becoming addicted to ouzo. Much
love Elizabeth

Alex and Nadia have for years had a summer retreat on Skiros, an
island in the Northern Sporades, and in the summer of 1982 they
were kind enough to lend it to Josephine and me for two weeks in
exchange for the loan to them of Josephine's house in Fulham. Neither
of us had been to Greece before so we arranged to spend a week on
the mainland visiting as many of the most famous sights as we could
fit in (the Parthenon, Delphi, Mycene and Epidaurus), but first there
was the adventure of Skiros.

Alex had told me that he had a tame taxi-driver called Andoni who
looked after the house for them when they were not there and who
would meet us at the port of Linaria and drive us to the house. All
we had to do was to send Andoni a telegram telling him the time of
our boat from Kimi (the mainland port, which we would reach by bus
from Athens). When he met us we were to tell him to take us first to a
shop in Linaria to stock up with provisions before we crossed the island.
"What languages does he understand?" I asked cautiously. "Well, only
Greek of course," Alex replied airily. Since Alex himself is fluent in at
least five languages, this did not seem to him to present any problem. It
did not seem quite so simple to me. Knowing Josephine's bad relationship with foreign languages, I could see that if anyone was going to con-
verse with Andoni in Greek it was going to have to be me. However,
there were still a few weeks to go, so I bought a BBC course of Modern
Greek for beginners and plunged in. The cassettes were accompanied
by a book called *Greek Language and People* seductively illustrated

with scenes from Greek life. Fortunately I had briefly studied Classical Greek at school and the alphabet came back to me quite readily. After that it was more of a struggle, but I have always enjoyed learning things (I was a terrible swot at school) so by the time we took our flight to Athens I felt I was quite competent to deal with the practical details of our holiday. I had even worked out an introductory sentence to be pronounced on meeting Andoni. Translated, it went something like: "You must be Andoni. How nice to meet you. I am Miss Paterson, this is Miss Pullein-Thompson. Please take us to the shop here before we go to the Blokhs' house." My confidence turned out to be misplaced.

Andoni was duly on the quayside at Linaria to meet us off the boat, looking like perfect casting for Zorba the Greek. I doubt if he had ever been an Adonis, even in his youth, and certainly, in middle age, the loss of several of his teeth had spoilt whatever good looks he had had. He was also, as we swiftly discovered, prejudiced against women (his wife Calliope being pretty but stupid) and against foreigners. His horror, therefore, when one of the two English women whom he had reluctantly agreed to take charge of during their visit to the island addressed him in some totally incomprehensible language was clearly mirrored on his face. My carefully composed Greek sentence obviously sounded like double dutch to him. It was Josephine who saved the day by speaking English loudly and clearly and waving her arms about in the accepted manner of the English abroad. He at once understood her meaning, if not her words, and took us to the general store so we were able to stock up on basic supplies in Linaria before being taken the seven or eight miles across the island to where the Blokhs' house awaited us.

It was built on the traditional island pattern, a white cube with a flat roof, most of which was taken up by a largish living room with a sleeping platform, reached by a ladder, at one end. There was also, opening off the entrance, a small kitchen, with a calor gas cooker, a lavatory with an unreliable flush, and a cold water shower. There was no electricity or telephone. We spent most of our time on the vine-shaded patio, went to bed early because of the difficulty of reading by lamplight, and did practically no cooking, becoming addicted to Greek salad, with fetta and delicious beef tomatoes. To do our shopping we had to walk the hot dusty mile or so to the little town of Skiros, with its narrow streets climbing up through white, black-roofed houses to the mediaeval citadel. Amongst these houses was the general store which housed the telephone. In subsequent years, when Alex used dutifully to ring the office from his summer month on Skiros, I was better able to understand the problems he had faced in getting through and to interpret the background noises of locals combining gossiping and marketing.

The first problem Josephine and I had to solve was which of us was going to sleep in the double bed on the sleeping platform, and which of us on the sofa down below. We tossed for the bed and I won. An unforeseen drawback of Josephine's sleeping arrangements was that a white kitten – one of the many cats on Skiros – which had immediately adopted us as a source of milk and entertainment, used to come into the house early in the morning and wake her by biting her nose. I slept undisturbed above. I did, however, have a problem owing to my height. When Alex had arranged with a local builder to build the house according to his specifications, he had had to return to Paris before the doorways were completed. He had therefore instructed the builder, by gesture, to leave a suitable clearance above the level of his head. The builder had faithfully obeyed his instructions, but had left the clearance over his own head. Alas he was a small man! I bumped my head so often during that holiday that I thought my brains would be permanently scrambled. Josephine was more the builder's height, so could pass unbent and unscathed through his doorways.

Cats were not the only animals that proliferated on the island. We were always prepared to repel an invasion by goats, which Alex had warned us would eat everything in sight if we allowed them near the house. There were also flocks of skinny sheep and plenty of donkeys and mules, their panniers laden with wood or produce from the fields. There were also the small sturdy horses, a breed native to Skiros, which were of particular interest to Josephine, who has ridden, broken, studied, loved and understood horses from an early age. Most of her books for younger readers are about children having adventures with ponies, and our holiday on Skiros provided the background for another one, "Save The Ponies", in which visiting English children help some local children to thwart a dastardly circus owner from Athens who plans to buy up horses from the poor farmers on the island, export them to the mainland and feed them to his lions and tigers. I was pleased to be in on the genesis of this exciting tale. We stumbled by chance on a race being held in a rough field outside the town of Skiros, in which children – mostly local boys – rode bareback , first in heats, and then in a fiercely contested final. The rules seemed rather vague – riders kept falling off and remounting – and many of the horses were rebellious and tried to go round the course backwards, but everyone seemed to be having a very enjoyable time. Inevitably one or two English girls, visitors to the island, had somehow got involved in the proceedings, and Josephine got into conversation with some of them and with a Greek girl from Athens who spoke good English. She also secured an introduction to the President of the Skirian Horse Society, who agreed to give her an interview. I went along as chaperone. Fortunately there was no need of an interpreter, since the President also spoke English. He was a thin dark man, a lawyer, who Alex afterwards told us had a reputation for shady dealing. He received us informally, barefoot, and was obviously delighted to talk about the horses, which were his passion. He was very firm that they were not ponies, and maintained that they were the models for the horses depicted in the frieze on the Parthenon. He told us that during the summer they were worked by their owners, the farmers in the cultivated north-east part of the island, but when winter approached they were driven to the barren southern section of the island and set loose there. After the winter they were rounded up at the spring at Nyphe, a beautiful spot at the narrow junction of the north and south of the island.

In the south part of the island also, set in a peaceful olive grove, is the movingly simple grave of Rupert Brooke (or "Brook", as he is known throughout the island and on the horrible Germanic statue in Skiros town which is supposed to represent him). We naturally wanted to see the grave and pay our respects, but were dependent upon Andoni for transport. This should not have presented a problem since Alex had arranged with Andoni that he would pass by the house in the mornings and pause to see if we wanted to be driven anywhere. Alex had also provided a map of the island with various favourite haunts of his and Nadia's marked on it. The system was that Andoni would hoot from the road, we would climb the rocky path up to the road and would consult with him over the map. However, every time we pointed to Rupert Brooke's grave he would shake his head and say something which, according to my dictionary, seemed to be "Too windy". Since the weather was perfectly calm, this did not seem a very valid objection and it was not until he finally gave in and took us there that we realised that the real reason for his reluctance was that the road to the grave was unmade up and therefore bad for the suspension of his taxi.

A far more serious cause of dispute between Andoni and us was entirely our fault. One of the excursions which Alex had recommended was to a beach on the north west side of the island, where he said we should arrange to spend a whole day, getting Andoni to drop us off there in the morning and collect us again in the evening. The first part of this plan went very well. Andoni dropped us off at a road junction near the beach and indicated the time that he would return to fetch us in the evening. We spent a delightful day swimming from the almost deserted sandy beach, lounging in the shade of the trees which fringed it, and lunching off fresh-caught fish in the taverna which was the only human habitation in sight. Full of sunshine and well-being, we made our leisurely way back to the coast road, determined not to keep Andoni waiting. Unfortunately the junction we waited at was not the one at which Andoni had dropped us. This was gradually born in on us as we waited, and waited ... and waited, until the sun set and we realised that Andoni was not going to come. We did the only possible thing and went back to the taverna to seek help. No-one there spoke any English, but they made it quite clear by signs that Andoni had been there looking for us, had waited a considerable time, no doubt drinking retsina and cursing us, and had then driven back across the island. The proprietor of the taverna, seeing our predicament, kindly telephoned Andoni (being a taxi driver, he fortunately had a telephone) and summoned him back. He came, looking thunderous, and drove us home in a smouldering silence.

It took some time for us to restore any sort of friendly relations with him. His low opinion of us was confirmed when he found that we had no taste for retsina, but preferred to quench our thirst during the daytime with the local beer (which, because of its name, lent itself to our frequent cry: "We must stop and have a Fix") and in the evenings to drink ouzo as an aperitif followed by Demestica (ordinary red wine). To Andoni this was heresy, but he did eventually unbend a little towards us and even, in after years, used to ask Alex how we were. He apparently referred to us as "the little goats", which seemed to us to be an ambiguous description, but Alex assured us that it was meant affectionately.

We certainly took away affectionate memories of our sun-soaked fortnight on the island. It was not all paradisal: Josephine trod on a sea-urchin and had to anoint her foot with olive oil to get the spikes out, and the wind changed halfway through our holiday and brought a plague of jelly-fish onto the beaches, which made swimming impossible, but these incidents provided useful background for the children's adventures in *Save The Ponies*, and they're not the ones that linger in the mind. Chiefly I remember the friendliness and patience of the shopkeepers in trying to discover what it was these eccentric foreign women were trying to ask for, and the restraint of the waiters in the cafes we patronised, who were apparently happy to leave us to consult our guide books for hours undisturbed by offers of service until we pronounced the magic word "*parakaló*" (please), which we belatedly discovered was the password to instant attention. Then there was the taxi driver (not Andoni) who stopped for us on the hot and dusty road from Skiros town, when we were trailing home with our shopping and when he heard where we were bound (*to spíti Blokh*, as I explained in my best Greek) would not let us pay.

I am sure the Skiriots are friendly to all visitors, in the best tradition of Greek hospitality, but we were certainly treated with extra kindness because of the respect and affection in which Alex and Nadia are held on the island.

Josephine arrived back at her house, which the Blokhs had vacated, to find a note of thanks from Alex with a puzzled postcript: "What is an airing cupboard?" In the instructions which Josephine had left for them, she had told them that that was where the switch for the hot water was located. It had not occurred to her, or to me, that the French plumbing system does not provide the householder with such a useful adjunct as an airing cupboard. Alex and Nadia had apparently searched the house high and low for this mysterious thing, but without success. They seemed to have enjoyed their stay in London nevertheless, though presumably surviving (like us on Skiros) on cold showers.

3

To KEVIN FITZGERALD   *Dakar*
Crossways, Chinnor, Oxon   *January 1993*

Dear Kevin,
We're being treated as V.I.P.'s (a turn-out of the presidential guard
in their fancy uniforms) because Senghor (now former President, but
still very much respected) is taking a personal interest in our confer-
ence. I think I would rather hear a griot *doing some story-telling than*
all these earnest African academics talking about the theory of oral
tradition, but I'm glad to be visiting Africa at last. We've been taken
to see the sad island of Goree, from which the slaves were shipped,
and are promised a trip to the south of the country after the conference.
Much love, Elizabeth

Throughout his presidency Per made great efforts to persuade African
writers to form PEN Centres. These efforts were unsuccessful at the
time because of the prevalence of dictatorships which made it dangerous, if not impossible, for writers to band together to support freedom
of speech. One of the African countries where, thanks to the benevolent presidency of the poet Léopold Sédar Senghor, there was an existing PEN Centre was Senegal, and in January 1983 International PEN
held a Seminar there on the importance of oral tradition. Most of
the African participants were bespectacled academics, who seemed
far-removed from the traditional story-tellers, the *griots*, who had
kept the oral tradition alive. Senghor, now succeeded as President of
Senegal by the immensely tall and thin Abdou Diouf, took a great
interest in the Seminar, which he presided over like a benevolent
schoolmaster. The non-African participants included, as well as Per
and Margareta, Alex and Nadia and myself, Peter and Barbara Elstob,
Francis King and Martin Tucker, a dark, bespectacled and friendly
professor from Long Island University, Editor of the American PEN
Newsletter and expert on African literature. We were staying in the
bland international surroundings of the Novotel with a watchman on
the gate to keep out intruders, but the moment we ventured into the
outside world we were brought face to face with the reality of local

life. One evening Francis, Martin and I set out to eat at a nearby restaurant, which turned out to be a hazardous enterprise because we were immediately surrounded, as if by a swarm of flies, by persistent salesmen trying to sell us leather goods and trinkets. Since the road was pot-holed and badly lit, it was impossible to make much speed to get away from them. Francis, who was the plumpest of us and the best-dressed, and so looked the most prosperous, tried unconvincingly to persuade them that he was a poor Russian with a lot of children and that they would do much better to turn their attention to Martin, who was a rich American. As we collapsed, laughing with relief, into the restaurant, we made the mistake of choosing a table on the patio, which was only protected from the street by a hedge, and no sooner had we settled ourselves than a black arm appeared over the hedge temptingly dangling an ivory bracelet!

Largely thanks to Senghor's patronage of the meeting, it was given generous coverage in the local press. In addition, many of the participants from neighbouring African countries promised that when they got home they would gather together other writers and set about founding PEN Centres. Elated by this success, Alex departed happily, with Nadia, to the beach resort of Ngor, where they would relax and swim and wait for the rest of us to join them after we had explored the area round the Casamance River, which they already knew from a previous visit. The Casamance is in the southern section of the country, which, due to the way Africa was carved up between the colonial powers, is separated from the north by a narrow tongue of land bordering the Gambia River which is part of the former British colony of The Gambia. Because of Per's high standing in Africa, he had been allotted a minivan, with a driver and a guide for this expedition and he and Margareta kindly made room for Francis, Martin and me in the back seat. Peter, according to his usual custom when abroad, had hired a car for Barbara and himself. So, in convoy, we drove south across the dry plains of northern Senegal. It was my first visit to Africa and I was disappointed with the scenery which, apart from the occasional rounded silhouette of a baobab tree, a few villages with fields of maize and millet and roadside stalls selling fruit, was flat and monotonous with not an animal in sight. The frontier with Gambia was chiefly marked by the change from French notices to English ones, from wine to tepid beer, and by the muddy brown expanse of the Gambia River which we crossed by a very crowded ferry. Then we were back in Senegal, but a very different countryside, heavily wooded, the villages set back from the road in clearings in the jungle. Our guide led us down a narrow path to one of these villages, where there were small pigs rooting in the dust between the huts. Peter, who is generally a great success with children, bent over to talk to a black baby, which promptly howled in terror at this bearded apparition – probably the first white man it had ever seen.

Somewhere en route we stopped for lunch at a very pleasant small hotel with a swimming pool. We did not have time for a swim as we had to get to Zigunchor, the principal town of Casamance, where we had booked rooms for the night. We arrived there in good time for dinner, only to find that there had been a muddle about our booking and there were not enough single rooms to accommodate Francis, Martin and me. There were two double-bedded rooms and one single reserved at the hotel we had chosen, and one double-bedded room at another hotel nearby. As we stood around, tired and dusty, debating what to do, Martin suddenly said: "If Elizabeth doesn't mind, I'd be happy to share with her". I was surprised by this offer, which seemed to me to come out of the blue from a man I only knew as an agreeable companion, but I was also flattered and, with the interested gaze of the rest of the party on both of us, it seemed no time to be coy. Everybody was relieved when I agreed since it meant they were all assured of beds. We had dinner together, and then Peter drove Martin and me off to our separate hotel and said he would come and collect us after breakfast the next morning. There was a display of African dancing laid on at our hotel and the sound of drumming went on into the early hours so that it seemed as if our relationship had begun in the heart of the jungle. It has lasted ever since.

Per meanwhile had discovered that he had left a bag containing his book (Margaret Drabble's latest novel) and all his traveller's cheques hanging from a hook in the lobby of the hotel where we had had lunch. He managed to get through to the hotel on the telephone and was greatly relieved to find that the bag was still where he had left it and the traveller's cheques untouched. He arranged to call in there on our way back north to collect the bag and was rather disconcerted when he did so to be told by the manager that "a lady" had telephoned to report his loss. He reckoned that his voice must have been falsetto with anxiety!

We only spent one night at the smart tourist hotels in Zigunchor. I find it difficult to retrace in my memory exactly where we went from there. I do recall a minor panic when we discovered that, although they had heard of credit cards in Zigunchor, they had not yet received the machines to deal with them, so our intention to pay our hotel bills with plastic were frustrated. Instead we had to queue for a long time in the bank to change what foreign currency we could muster. Having managed to overcome that problem, we made an excursion to Karabane, an island in the Casamance River which was an early off-shore trading base and the first French toehold in the territory. It was a peaceful, largely deserted, place, where the large, half-ruined Breton-style church and some handsome crumbling houses were the only traces left of its mercantile past. I also have, as proof of our other activities, some idyllic photographs of Peter, Per and Martin, in their bathing trunks, sitting in a beached dug-out canoe, roasting in the sun. I kept discreetly in the shade, trying to avoid turning lobster-red. We went back to Zigunchor for one more night and stayed in the only accommodation we could find, a genuinely African hotel, where Martin and I had a large room very inadequately lit and none too clean in the corners. However the dinner which we were served in the open courtyard of the hotel was unexpectedly good.

We had decided to spend a night on our way back in Banjul, the capital of The Gambia, but had not decided which hotel to stay at. We were therefore rather worried when our convoy became divided. Peter, with his usual insouciance about maps, driving his hired car, with Barbara and Francis (who had decided that it might be more comfortable than the minivan) on board, deviated from our route and disappeared from our ken. We, in our minivan, arrived in Banjul according to plan, booked ourselves in at the largest and smartest beachside hotel, and sat down to dinner. We were not greatly worried about the Elstob party because we knew Peter's talent for survival against any odds. I also reassured the others that, since it had been my experience that Francis had an uncanny instinct for the best res-taurant in any town anywhere in the world and, since we had undoubtedly chosen the best hotel in Banjul, he and the Elstobs would be sure to be joining us shortly. This turned out to be the case.

The next morning Per, intellectually curious as always, got up early and went round the lounging chairs by the pool making a survey of the books which our fellow guests (mostly English middle management and their wives) had put out to bag their places. Not surprisingly, there was no Margaret Drabble here. Arthur Hailey and Jackie Collins were the favourites.

We lounged by the pool ourselves for a bit before continuing our journey north to join the Blokhs in their holiday paradise at Ngor. There we were assigned thatched bedroom huts among the palm trees by the beach, and met for meals at the central restaurant, also with a thatched roof. A pair of tame pelicans paraded the beach touting for food from the bathers and, at our first dinner in the restaurant, Alex and Nadia, who are great cat-lovers, were enchanted when an opened flap on the sideboard revealed a cat and a family of kittens.

While we had been in Casamance Alex had been taking a course in sailboarding. Sadly he had not made much progress so that he spent more time falling off his board than standing on it. He showed his strength of character by persevering undeterred by all these mishaps. Per, rather unkindly, waded into the sea with his camera to take a close-up shot of Alex falling off his sail-board for the umpteenth time.

After Ngor we all went our separate ways, Martin leaving first, in the middle of our farewell lobster dinner, to catch his plane back to The States. By that time I had picked up some African virus and was feeling dizzy and sick on the flight back to London, so I was glad to have Francis' sympathetic company. Fortunately the virus was only a mild one and by the time my doctor had got the result of my blood test, which showed that I had indeed had a virus, I had recovered.

4

To KEVIN FITZGERALD   *Venice*
Crossways, Chinnor, Oxon   *May 1983*

Dear Kevin,
This promises to be the dottiest of all the dotty PEN meetings I've
attended, but since we're staying in the Hotel Europa and crossing to
the Island of San Giorgio Maggiore to hold our discussions in the
Fondazione Cini, it's also delightful. The organiser is Contessa Mimy
Piovene, who has single-handedly brought back Italian PEN from the
dead and (regardless of the fact that she is Milanese, not Venetian)
seems to be organising – or disorganising – this Conference single-
handedly also. She's a remarkable character. I'll tell you more about
her when we meet. Much love, Elizabeth

Mimy Piovene was a welcome addition to the large cast of notable
characters in PEN Her memory is preserved to this day in our part
of Fulham since Josephine has named her little blue Fiat after her,
partly because of its Italian extraction, but also because it carries a
suggestion of Mimy's small, plump figure, trotting along on very high
heels. Mimy made no claim to be a writer herself, but she had the
distinction of being the widow of the novelist Guido Piovene and was
the only person with the money and the determination to get Italian
PEN going again after many years in limbo. She used to come to King
Street from the Savoy, where she stayed when she was in London,
expensively dressed in furs, and pay the Italian Centre's dues in money
which obviously came from her own pocket. I remember when she
came to one of my Writers' Day parties, she made me nervous by
casting an assessing eye over my dress, making me aware that I was
probably bulging in the wrong places, and then relieved me with a
friendly nod of approval.

To undertake to organise a PEN Conference in Venice only a year
after the Italian Centre had been revived, with no committee to help
her and with no base in Venice, was a mad enterprise which only
someone with Mimy's *chutzpah* would have undertaken. Reporting
on the Conference to the Congress in Caracas which succeeded it in

September 1983, Per said that Mimy's "forceful and buoyant personality had given the meeting a strong personal profile." It certainly did and it succeeded triumphantly, but the start was alarming. Alex and I arrived the day before the other participants, to find that the delegates' folders were all in a jumble in Mimy's room at the Europa amongst her tights and curlers. We brought them all down to the hotel lobby where, ably assisted by Andrew Graham-Yooll, who had now replaced John Peet as Press Officer, we tried to sort them into some kind of order. Lavinia, an old hand at these occasions, stood guard over us and repelled other early-arriving delegates who wanted to pester us with questions. Mimy meanwhile was meeting arrivals at the airport, standing at the prow of the hotel boat like a figurehead, whilst the two Japanese delegates, exhausted from their long journey, sat slumped in a corner of the lobby, waiting for her to return and sort out their hotel bookings.

When Mimy finally returned with her latest cargo of arrivals Alex called her attention to the depressed Japanese. The receptionist was all compliance ("Piacere, Contessa . . ."), but could only produce one double room for the two delegates to share. It fell to Alex to put this to the Japanese, and he, assuming that the taller of the two was the more important, asked him if he would mind sharing a room with his colleague. It was immediately apparent that Alex was wrong and it was the shorter one who was higher in the pecking order. Asked by the taller one if he would mind sharing, he said "Yes" with great decision. It was left to Mimy to cut the Gordian knot by dispatching them both to another hotel on the Lido.

The theme of the Congress was "Venice in Literary Sensibility" and Stephen Spender, who was one of the guests of honour, gave a paper which appropriately included a reading of Browning's "A Tocatta of Galuppi's":

"What, they lived once thus at Venice where the merchants were the
kings,
Where St. Mark's is, where the Doges used to wed the sea with rings? . . .
Dear dead women with such hair, too – what's become of all the gold
Used to hang and brush their bosoms? I feel chilly and grown old."

He read it beautifully without giving any hint that he was distracted by the odd behaviour of his fellow-speaker, Giorgio Bassani, who got up from his seat and peered over Stephen's shoulder while he was speaking.

Stephen unwittingly raised my status in the eyes of the foreign delegations by coming to sit with me one morning at breakfast at a table for two. I think he really only saw me as a useful opener of the hotel's tiresome little plastic honey pots which defeated his clumsy fingers.

Venice worked its magic on the sessions of the Assembly of Delegates, which were peaceful and constructive. Even an American Centre resolution urging the release from a Soviet prison of the poet Irina Ratushinskaya drew no opposition from the Eastern European delegations. Henryk Keisch had been appeased by finally getting a respectable majority for a resolution in favour of nuclear disarmament, similar to the one which had been voted down at a previous meeting on the grounds that nuclear disarmament was a matter of general concern, not specific to writers. The Venice resolution was drafted as an appeal to the Co-Chairmen of the Disarmament Conference at Geneva and established its relevance to PEN by the inclusion of the clause: "Convinced that the international intellectual co-operation which PEN exists to serve can only be assured and developed in a climate of confidence such as is being compromised by the arms race". It was in the course of the discussion of this resolution that the Slovene delegate, Milos Mikeln, first suggested the establishment of the PEN Writers for Peace Committee, of which he later became the first Chairman and which has met annually at Bled ever since.

The Venice Conference, however, is more likely to be remembered by its participants for the eccentric brilliance of its parties. One unfortunate Contessa, a friend of Mimy's with an ancient palazzo, had been persuaded to give a party for the delegates on Mimy's airy assurance that there would only be about forty of us. The actual number was twice that, and our hostess was obviously panic-stricken that the floors might give way or the whole palazzo sink into the Grand Canal.

We also had a delightful excursion to Vicenza, where we were entertained at the Villa Vilmarana (known as *dei Nani* because of the statues of dwarfs which crown its outer walls) which was owned by another of Mimy's friends. Since the Villa Vilmarana is outside Vicenza the bus which had brought us from Venice took us on there, but could not negotiate the narrow lane leading down to it from the main road, so we had to get out and walk. It was raining, but it was only a short distance and we most of us felt that getting a little wet was a small price to pay for the privilege of seeing this villa, with its beautiful Tiepolo frescoes, at a time when it was closed to the general public. The French ladies, however, of "les Amis du PEN" (wealthy supporters of *le Pen Club* who enjoyed the touristic aspect of the organisation rather than the literary) were very unhappy to have their coiffures ruined and made Alex feel that it was entirely his fault for not arranging matters better.

*

To KEVIN FITZGERALD   *Caracas*
Crossways, Chinnor, Oxon   *September 1983*

Dear Kevin,
I thought that Venezuela just consisted of oil wells and was the last
place in the world I wanted to visit, but I'm finding Caracas very
enjoyable. The weather is pleasant, the people most hospitable
and, although the city is ultra-modern with skyscrapers and super-
highways it's also full of trees, parks and gardens and is still centered
on the handsome Plaza Bolívar, where sloths pursue their peaceful
lifestyle amongst the trees – very restful to watch since they take half
an hour to move from one branch to another. After the Congress,
dauntless explorers that we are, we're off to the Canaima National
Park in the Guyana Highlands, south of the Orinoco. Much love,
Elizabeth

The President of Venezuelan PEN, José Ramon Medina, small, bespectacled, always dressed in a suit and with his hair immaculately sleeked
back, looked much more like a wealthy and successful businessman
than a writer. He had attended a few International PEN meetings,
but, since Spanish was his only language, had never spoken in the
Assembly except to put the invitation for the Caracas Congress. However on his home ground it was obvious that he was a man of power
and influence; the Congress organisation was smooth and efficient
and the parties lavish. One thing he could not organise was the party
given for us by the President of Venezuela. Our buses delivered us
punctually and, dressed in our best, we trooped into the marquee
where it was to be held, which was in the beautiful garden of La
Casona, the President's official residence, only to find that the tables
laden with food and drink were being guarded by heavily-armed soldiers, who kept us at bay for half an hour whilst we waited for the
President to arrive. I had often thought that only sub-machine-guns
would keep PEN delegates from their food, but had never before had
a chance to test this theory! When the President finally arrived, a big,
burly, grey-haired man with a moustache, who, unusually for a Latin
American Head of State, had been democratically elected and was an
academic, he was charming. We were all led up to be introduced to
him individually by José Ramon and photographed shaking hands
with him. Then at last to the food and drink, which was superb. The
delicious fruit cocktails were very deceptive, since they slid down so

easily that one was tempted to drink a lot of them, only discovering afterwards their high alcoholic content.

On another evening Per, Peter and I enjoyed Venezuelan hospitality at a different level. Coming out onto the street from a party in the centre of Caracas, we decided to try to find a good fish restaurant. Peter, as the Spanish speaker, stopped a passer-by and asked him to direct us. He turned out to be a train driver, a young man who, although he was on his way home to his wife, immediately changed his plans; he said he knew just the place and would take us there. He summoned a taxi and we were driven off for some distance to a restaurant which was evidently owned by a friend of his. There he threw his weight about, summoning waiters and recommending dishes. Clearly he was gaining kudos by bringing three foreigners to the restaurant. The food was good, but we were worried about what trouble he would get into with his wife when he eventually got home and how, without damaging his pride, we were going to manage to pay for the meal. Peter solved the latter problem by paying the bill when our host had gone to the lavatory and then telling him that it was an unbreakable English custom that the oldest man present always paid for the meal. We parted with many expressions of undying friendship. What he told his wife we shall never know.

Because of the cost of travel to Venezuela, there were fewer than usual delegates from European Centres in Caracas. One who did make it, against heavy odds, was the President of Icelandic PEN, Thor Vilhjálmsson. Thor, with his bush of white hair, white beard and bright blue eyes, looks like a sea captain, but is one of the most distinguished poets in Scandinavia. He also, when he's away from home, drinks heavily and seems always to be charmingly detached from reality so that if he were indeed a sea captain, his navigation would be very questionable. His journey to Caracas had been more than usually haphazard since he had had his passport stolen in London en route and had to arouse the long-suffering Icelandic Ambassador in the early hours of the morning to solve the problem. Somehow, nonetheless, he managed to arrive in Caracas, admittedly a couple of days late and looking dazed, as if he had just landed from outer space. He did arrive in time, however, to contribute to a general discussion which was held in the Assembly on how the different Centres operated. He described how when he had met Peter at the Unesco Conference in Belgrade a few years previously Peter, then International Secretary, had told him that he should take over Icelandic PEN, which was in danger of being liquidated because it was so inactive. Thor had replied that the President of the Centre was a very fine man and a good friend of his so he would have to be tactful. He had, however, managed in due time to stage a *coup d'état* and the Icelandic Centre was now very lively. The only problem, he complained, was that he now seemed to be losing the poets on his committee to the new-born craze for the cinema in Iceland and the Secretary was wildly making a samurai film in some deserted part of the country so that he, Thor, had to run the Centre in addition to all his other work.

Earlier, in an unusual development, two resolutions addressed to Western democracies had been discussed in the Assembly. The first was Josephine's brainchild. It had come to the attention of English PEN that, as a result of the Falklands War, U.K. Customs had impounded publications sent from Argentina. A Latin American Congress had seemed the ideal opportunity to get a resolution passed condemning this breach of the Florence Agreement on the free importation of educational, scientific and cultural material. However, thanks to Josephine's efficient liaison with the British Embassy in Caracas, she was able to tell the Assembly that two days previously the Minister of State for Trade had made a statement in the House of Commons in which he had said that books would henceforth be exempted from the general ban on material from Argentina and that this exemption would be retrospective. The English Centre resolution was therefore withdrawn to general applause.

The second resolution came from the Dutch Centre and called upon the U.S. Congress to repeal the clause in the McCarran Walter Act, which forbade entry to the U.S. to all aliens who were members of communist or anarchist organisations, which included such writers as Gabriel Garcia Marquez, Mahmoud Darwish and Dario Fo. Mimy Piovene took exception to the resolution because of its mention of Dario Fo, who, in her opinion, was not a writer, but a cabaret actor and a propagandising communist who therefore should be excluded from the United States. This offended the Bulgarian delegation and roused Per, from the Chair, to say that in his opinion Dario Fo was one of the great dramatists of the world. Joseph Strelka (the very Right Wing and pro-American Austrian delegate), wanted to amend the resolution to include the Soviet Union, Poland and Czechoslovakia. Per dealt briskly with this proposal, attacking the feeling which some delegates had that in every resolution there should be a balance between the two political camps. On the contrary every delegation should be free to submit resolutions concerning any country they wished provided these had to do with violations of the PEN Charter. He commented that we all had our subjective grades of heat in hell, but we must keep to resolutions citing very specific violations and addressed to specific governments.

The American Centre strongly supported the Dutch resolution, saying that the McCarran Walter Act was a hang-over from the McCarthy era, and the resolution was carried nem. con., with three abstentions.

The other matter which once more greatly exercised the Assembly was the deplorable situation of the PE.N. Centre in Poland, where life was becoming increasingly difficult because of the disastrous economic situation and particularly difficult for writers because of the government's tightening grip on cultural life. Now the government had, quite illegally, dissolved the Polish PEN Board and appointed a caretaker Board of their own. This was the first time any government had interfered in the internal affairs of a PEN Centre and it aroused a great deal of indignation amongst the delegates. Messages had been received both from Juliusz Zulawski, the President of Polish PEN, in Warsaw, and from Wladyslaw Bartoszewski, the Secretary, in Germany, urging International PEN not to recognise the caretaker Board.

Both Per and Alex advised that nothing dramatic or sensational should be done until there had been time for reflection, so a resolution was eventually passed, with only two abstentions (the Bulgarian and GDR delegations), protesting against the Polish government's action and requesting them to re-establish the PEN Board so that it could call a meeting of the membership either to renew its mandate or elect a new Board. Meanwhile aid was to be channelled to Polish PEN by the Liaison Committee which had been appointed in Venice.

*

When the Congress proceedings had duly been concluded a small group of us set off for a trip to the Canaima National Park in the Guyana Highlands, near the border with Brazil. We travelled by a small local plane and when we gathered on the tarmac Josephine, Tony, Peter and I were informally dressed, but Alex for some reason was immaculate in a suit, carnation in buttonhole and carrying a rolled umbrella. Josephine teased him that in an English school story he would have been cast as the overdressed sissy French boy, a description which he took in good part!

Our flight to Canaima took us past Angel Falls which, although not nearly as impressive in bulk as the Victoria Falls or Niagara, are the highest in the world, falling 3,200 feet. As our pilot described to us how the Falls had been discovered in 1935 by an American bush pilot, Jimmy Angel, who was searching for gold, all of us got up and went over to the side of the aircraft from which we could get the best view. This made the plane dip wildly to one side and we wondered if we were going to join the other wrecked aircraft which we could see scattered about the base of the Falls.

Apparently when Jimmy Angel landed on one of the flat-topped mountains characteristic of this area, Auyán-tepui, his plane got stuck in the mud and he had to cut his way out through a vast unmapped jungle. He did manage to get home, but we were told of another character, a recluse, thought to be a Polish refugee, who had made his home in the jungle. Like the Yeti, various sightings of him had been reported. What he lived on was not clear, but I suppose there is plenty of fruit there, and perhaps there are monkeys, although we did not see any.

When we got to the Campamiento Canaima we found it was beautifully situated on a lagoon, surrounded by a sandy beach, into which the Carrao River (a tributary of the Orinoco) tumbles over seven small waterfalls. We each had a bedroom hut with its own shower and loo, and there was a central hut where we fed – largely on beans as far as I can remember. We stayed there for three days and on one of those days took an excursion down the river to a beauty spot called the Isla Orquidea, where we had a beach barbecue, concluding, surprisingly, with fruit salad eaten out of the tin. The start of our excursion was delayed by Peter, who, bolshie as ever, refused to put on a life-jacket. We had already set out when the Indian at the helm of our boat spotted this omission and returned us to the jetty, where he stood over Peter while he meekly gave in and donned the life-jacket he had scorned.

Peter made up for this uncharacteristic submissiveness later on when we had stopped for lunch by insisting on swimming in the middle of the river whilst the rest of us, having been told by our guides that there were dangerous currents further out, were splashing about in the shallows. "Come out here, Josephine and Elizabeth", he cried, "It's much nicer", but we wisely ignored him. On the way down to our picnic spot we had disembarked at the foot of one of the waterfalls in this land of waterfalls to watch our Indian guides perform their party trick of diving from the top of the fall into the pool at its foot. Some of the young men in our party felt challenged to copy them and I was afraid Peter might do the same, but he confined himself to climbing to the top and coming down the same way.

It was an idyllic day. The Isla Orquidea lived up to its name, and I've got a photograph of Josephine and Alex admiring one of the orchids hanging down from a tree. Except that they're both wearing swim suits, they look rather like Adam and Eve in the Garden of Eden. I also took a photograph of Peter and Tony standing by our beached dugout canoe, each holding a paddle. Since the outboard motor is not visible, they look like dauntless explorers who have penetrated the trackless jungle alone and unaided.

5

KEVIN FITZGERALD   *Tokyo*
Chinnor, Crossways, Oxon   *May, 1984*

Dear Kevin,
This is the most splendid Congress yet – magnificent parties and more
than 600 participants. Our hotel is an enormously high skyscraper,
but the lifts function with Japanese efficiency and bear one aloft at
lightning speed. Even in the Shinjuku Gardens, where we went to find
peace and tranquillity among the azaleas, there were PEN delegates
behind every bush! Much love, Elizabeth

The theme of the Tokyo Congress was a very serious one: "Literature
in the Nuclear Age. Why Do We Write?", but I chiefly remember it
for various less weighty reasons.

A prominent PEN delegate who had always hitherto appeared at
Congresses accompanied by a much younger girl friend, a docile,
doe-eyed beauty, was this time firmly accompanied by his wife. Unfortunately Pavel Tigrid, who knew the girl friend well from other Congresses, but had never met the wife, greeted the delegate within his
wife's hearing by asking affectionately after the girl. I had always
thought that the couple had a "civilised" arrangement whereby the
wife pursued her own interests and turned a blind eye to what her
husband did when abroad. I was wrong, and the repercussions of the
brick Pavel had dropped reverberated round the Congress and beyond.
The marriage held, but the girl friend was utterly banished.

Pavel never came to a Congress again until his brief appearance as
Minister of Culture at the Prague Congress ten years later. His absence,
however, was certainly not due to embarrassment at his *faux pas*, but
because, with the waning of the Cold War, he no longer felt it necessary to pursue his favourite sport of dropping salt on the tails of the
delegates from Eastern Europe. Since his quarrels with Peter were now
too in the past, I missed the stimulus he provided in the Assembly.

In the continuing saga of Polish PEN the Centre had, early in 1984,
at the request of the legitimate Board, been declared dormant. It was
unanimously agreed in the Tokyo Assembly that Per, as International

President, should accept an invitation he had received from the Polish Minister of Culture to go to Warsaw to meet with Polish writers of all shades of opinion and with government officials in order to get a clearer view of the prevailing situation. Meanwhile some Polish PEN members who had turned up in Tokyo, in spite of having been told that they could not be considered as official delegates of the Centre, were generally regarded with suspicion as lick-spittles to the Polish Government.

When we had concluded the Congress business in Tokyo with due pomp and ceremony, we all boarded the Bullet Train to Kyoto. Our enjoyment of the train's spectacular speed was tempered by the fear of not being able to get off at Kyoto in the two minutes allowed. René Tavernier (newly elected an International Vice-President) was so determined that whoever else got left on the train it should not be the French delegation that he had them all marshalled and standing in the aisle well before our arrival at the station. Spurred on no doubt by a determination not to be left standing by the French, the rest of us somehow managed to get ourselves and our luggage off the train in time.

In Kyoto we were delighted by the many beautiful temples and gardens, but I was surprised to find that the Japanese, with their strong sense of order and beauty, had allowed the rest of the city to degenerate into a messy urban sprawl. There seemed to be no such thing as town planning.

The chief social event of our stay was thanks to Francis, who, having worked for The British Council in Japan for several years, had many friends there. Two of these, now professors, invited him to bring a party to a tea house and I was lucky enough to be included, together with Per and Margareta, Alex and Nadia and Peter. We sat on the floor round a low table, with our hosts one at either end. I was placed next to Francis, who explained to me in an undertone that the young girls who were entertaining us were *maikos* (apprentice geishas) since the cost of hiring full-blown geishas would have been prohibitive. Their hair was dressed very elaborately, with jewelled combs, but the white make-up with which their faces were plastered did not succeed in concealing their adolescent pimples. After serving us with saki and refreshments they did a graceful dance, starting in a diagonal line with their backs to us because, as Francis explained to me, the Japanese consider the back of the neck to be the most erotic part of the body. He went on to say that when the *maikos* reached puberty they would each be chosen by a wealthy patron, who would deflower them, which would be their rite of passage to becoming geishas.

Unfortunately Alex was seated too far away to benefit from

Francis's explanation and, his intellectual curiosity being aroused, he asked one of our hosts: "How do maikos become geishas? Do they have to pass some kind of examination?". It was as if a shutter had been drawn down over the faces of our hosts and there was an uneasy silence until someone hastily changed the subject. In the taxi going back to our hotel Nadia said she was sorry she had not been near enough to Alex to kick him.

The hostess at the tea house was a retired geisha who had been around at the time of the last Tokyo Congress, in 1957, and she recited to us a haiku she had written on that occasion.

*

After Kyoto a privileged few of us set off for a tour of China as guests of the Mainland Chinese PEN Centres. It amused me that English should be the common language of our disparate group, although I was the only English member amongst the ten of us. The others were: two Swedes (Per and Margareta), two French (Alex and Nadia), two Dutch (Martin Mooij and his wife), two Venezuelans (Jose Ramon Medina and his wife), and our guide Jin Jianfan (Executive Secretary of the China PEN Centre in Beijing).

I think it was in the space of a week that we fitted in the principal sights in and around Beijing (the Forbidden City, the Summer Palace and a trip to the Great Wall), the imperial tombs at Xian, and Shanghai, which made me feel at home with its small replica of Big Ben down on the waterfront of the Bund. As Nadia said, we came to look more and more like a group of refugees, always packing up and waiting beside our pile of luggage to be moved on to the next place. Wherever we went the locals all stopped whatever they were doing and turned to stare at us as if we were animals in a zoo. The writers we met, on the other hand, were invariably charming and hospitable. I particularly remember the plump and smiling Secretary of the Beijing Centre, Mr. Bi, and the pipe-smoking playwright, Du Xuan, who was President of the Shanghai PEN Centre and spoke impeccable English.

Jin Jianfan was a very conscientious guide. He told us that his father had a restaurant in Shanghai and Jianfan had obviously risen in the world by going to Beijing and getting a job with PEN. Whether or not he was also employed by the government was a debatable point.

Undoubtedly the most spectacular sight of our tour was the terra-cotta army at Xian. These life-size figures of cavalrymen which had been placed in ranks over the tomb of one of the emperors were then still in process of being excavated, but we were able to walk round the trench and look down on them where they lay in disarray as if they had fallen on a battlefield. It was a curiously moving experience and well worth enduring the privations of The People's Hotel at Xian, a ramshackle and dirty building, where we were served revolting food. As Per battled with the kitchen to get a lightly-boiled egg instead of the cannon balls they supplied, Alex said whimsically: "Just think of all those merchants toiling for thousands of miles along the Great Silk Road from Venice to Xian to find themselves at The People's Hotel"!

At the end of our Chinese tour we split up: Per and Margareta and the Mooijs to return to Europe, the Ramon Medinas to go to India, and Alex and Nadia and I to go to Korea as guests of Korean PEN.

This was the first time Alex had visited Korea since 1948, when he had been there as part of a U.N. mission and had fallen in love with the country and its people, including one particular Korean girl. When he practised some of his rusty Korean on Miss Suh, the delightful girl who was attached to us as our guide, she giggled and was eventually induced to explain that the language he was using was pillow talk. He could not get over the miraculous change in the country from the muddy cart-tracks and primitive housing he had known to the highly industrialised society that had grown up since the Korean War. I felt that our hosts were not entirely pleased to be reminded so often of how primitive their life had been, but they were far too polite to say so.

Miss Suh took us to Kyongju and some of the beauty spots around it that I had seen in 1970. We also spent a day or two in Seoul and I was taken to see Miss Moh, who had had a stroke and was a sadly diminished figure. She held my hand and was rather tearful, but was pleased when I reminisced about the splendid time we had had in 1970, and her eyes lit up when I mentioned David.

Our principal hostess was Mrs. Chun Sook-hee, the President of Korean PEN, a delightfully unassuming woman, but nevertheless one of great influence. She, together with Miss Moh and Mrs. Cho, had founded the Korean PEN. Mrs. Cho Kyung-hee, a plump and bustling figure who reminded me of Mrs. Tiggywinkle, perhaps because of her spiky haircut and the benevolent twinkle in her eye, was also a powerful woman, now Minister of Culture. She very generously insisted on arranging for Nadia and me to have outfits made for us by Mr. Kim, *the* haute couturier of South Korea. She took us personally to his salon, where, entirely dressed in white, he presided over a bevy of assistants. Whereas Nadia, with her elegance of figure and dress, was in her element, I, who had only ever bought clothes off the peg, was totally unnerved by the whole ambience. Mrs. Cho, sensing my alarm as we watched Nadia make her choice amongst the various fashion plate designs offered to her, lent across and patted my knee. "You and I, my dear", she said "are working women who like sensible clothes". I was, as with other Korean friends, enchanted by her ready comprehension. In the end I came away with a very beautiful brown velvet evening jacket laced with gold thread.

From Korea we went on to Bangkok and I once more entered the sort of fantasy land which I had briefly experienced at the Minister of Defence's beach house at Batangas in The Philippines in 1970. This time it was the more sophisticated delights of the Oriental Hotel at Bangkok, deservedly famed as one of the great hotels of the world. We were guests there by courtesy of the management because the Thai PEN Centre were negotiating the possibility of holding a Congress at the hotel in the future. Sadly, this never came about, but I was glad to get a taste of such luxury as I would never normally have experienced.

When I was shown up to my suite I barely had time to admire the view over the river from the big bay window in the sitting-room before there was a ring on the door-bell and a magnificent display of flowers and fruit was wheeled in. Then, just as I was stripping off to have a shower before going out to meet the Thai PEN Committee for dinner, there was another ring and another smiling functionary appeared with a packet of the hotel letter head with my name embossed on it in gold lettering.

I felt I could have spent days living in this cosseted atmosphere, but, sadly, I had to leave the next day to fly back to London and real life. After travelling round in a group for so long I felt rather bereft when I had said goodbye to Alex and Nadia (who were going to the coast for a few days) and set off for the airport on my own. Then, as I was queuing up at the check-in, who should I see at another check-in desk, surrounded by a mound of luggage, but the trim figure of José Ramon Medina. Presumably he and his wife were on their way back from their Indian tour. Since I have no Spanish and he no English, we could not communicate other than by beaming smiles, but he seemed as glad to see me as I was to see him.

*

Back in London there was a welcome six-month interval before we had to organise the November meeting of the Assembly of Delegates.

This gap was particularly welcome to me because I was moving house from Rosebury Road, where I had lived for ten years, to a smaller, terrace house next to Josephine's in Knivet Road which I had acquired at the asking price thanks to Josephine's vigilance in telling me that it was coming on the market even before the agents' board went up. This was also in Fulham, but much more conveniently situated for public transport.

The difficulty of transport to and from Rosebury Road had almost caused an international incident when I had celebrated my last Writers' Day party there in March of that year. I had had a larger than usual number of foreign guests, since, as well as the habitués, Per and Margareta, Alex and Nadia, René Tavernier and Solange Fasquelle (René's mistress of many years standing and herself later President of French PEN), there were also Iván Boldizsár (from Hungarian PEN) and Milos Mikeln (from Slovene PEN). At the end of the party they had all decided not to wait for me to call minicabs to get them back to their different hotels, but to pick up taxis on the Wandsworth Bridge Road. Milos crossing over to the other side of the road, was the first to be successful and, instead of offering to share his taxi, waved cheerfully to his frustrated colleagues as he drove away.

*

The chief matter discussed at the November meeting of the Assembly of Delegates was once more the situation of Polish PEN and this gave rise to a very characteristic PEN debate.

Per had just returned from a visit to Warsaw at the invitation of the Minister of Culture, during which, as well as meetings with the legitimate Board of Polish PEN and representatives of the new (government-appointed) Writers' Union and National Council of Culture, he had had an interview of an hour and twenty minutes with the President of Poland, General Jaruzelski. This had taken place at the President's request, which Per commented was a measure of the esteem in which International PEN was held by the Polish Government and its eagerness to solve the present conflict between the old and new Boards of Polish PEN so that the Centre's international links could be resumed. Per had remained uncompromising on International PEN's stipulation that until the legitimate Board was reinstated the Centre would continue to be regarded as dormant.

It was a tribute to the way in which Per had conducted these tricky negotiations that even Bob den Doolaard, always alert for signs of compromise with the communist authorities, congratulated him on never allowing himself to be tripped up into making any statement which compromised the PEN Charter. Although in Poland he had been treated like visiting royalty, he had allowed it all to flow over him like water off a duck's back. Bob felt obliged to point out, however, that the official Polish news agency, PAP, had given a very one-sided picture of Per's activities and some people in Poland might have gained the impression that he was a duck that was swimming in government waters. Taking up Bob's metaphor with obvious relish, Per replied that he felt that he had not only not compromised the PEN Charter, but had also managed to swim sometimes on the water like a duck, sometimes under it like a fish, and sometimes to soar above it like an eagle.

His report was accepted by general acclaim.

Concluding the meeting, he commented that it must be evident to the delegates that the International Secretariat could not be accused of living in excessive luxury. He felt that the disordered intimacy of the Africa Centre suited the life of PEN, which tended to be very disordered, sometimes in castles, sometimes in cellars. He looked forward to their next meeting, which was to be in San Marino, the oldest republic in Europe.

6

To KEVIN FITZGERALD   *San Marino*
Crossways, Chinnor, Oxon   *May 1985*

Dear Kevin,
Alex has somehow charmed the San Marino representative at Unesco
into hosting a meeting for us in this delightful hill-top republic which
is entirely surrounded by Italy. There's no PEN Centre and I doubt
if there are any writers. Everyone we meet seems to be a Minister in
the government. The Foreign Minister runs a travel agency in the main
street and it is rumoured that the plump and motherly Minister of
Tourism was seen dusting the Town Hall before our Welcome Recep-
tion! Much love, Elizabeth

It was difficult to give our attention to serious business in the light-
hearted atmosphere of San Marino, which was more suited to the discussion of children's literature, which was the theme of the literary
sessions. The Assembly was enlivened, however, by an outburst of rage
from Theophilos Frangopoulos, the hulking, scowling delegate from
Greek PEN, who had been sent by his Centre to express their extreme
displeasure at a resolution adopted at the London meeting which criti-
cised the Greek government for their policy of suppressing the language
and culture of the Macedonian minority in Greece. This had been submitted by the Croatian PEN, no doubt at the request of the Macedonian
Centre in Skopje who wanted to show solidarity with their fellow-
Macedonians across the border. Greek PEN utterly denied the existence
of Macedonians in Greece and Mr. Frangopoulos, although declaring
that it was not his Centre's intention to bring up Balkan quarrels,
immediately proceeded to do so by saying that Greek PEN could not
"harbour any feelings of good will or friendliness towards those PEN
Centres which had raised an issue which had been felt to be wounding
to their nation". Therefore, in addition to not recognising the offending
resolution as being in any way binding on them, they would not participate in any international meetings taking place in Yugoslavia and would
discontinue their collaboration with other Balkan PEN Centres as long
as the Yugoslav PEN's were also taking part.

This outburst provoked an astonished and pained response from all the Yugoslav delegates present, one of whom (the Croatian, Predrag Matvejevic) described it as more like paramilitary behaviour. It also brought a sharp rap over the knuckles from the Chair. Per said that for one Centre to break off relations with others was unheard of in PEN and ran counter to the Charter. No Centre could be allowed to boycott international meetings. If Greek PEN found the Croatian resolution deplorable they must produce arguments against it and, if they could not get it changed, they must accept it or leave PEN. He instructed Frangopoulos to report his words to the Greek PEN Board. Frangopolous stormed out of the meeting muttering imprecations. I never discovered what he wrote. He may possibly have been a poet, but at that moment he only lacked a dagger in his belt to complete his likeness to a bandit from the mountains.

The plausible young man from Jordan was certainly a poet, or purported to be. He came as an observer, anxious to start a PEN Centre in Amman. He was well-equipped with miniature Jordanian flags, which he distributed amongst the delegates, and was charmingly attentive to the older women. He had only managed to get seventeen Jordanian writers to sign the Charter instead of the requisite minimum of twenty, but explained convincingly that this was because of the twenty-one writers had originally signed four had subsequently lost their nerve and withdrawn their signatures. This was because freedom of expression was not a welcome concept in Jordan. He pleaded for the PEN rules to be bent to admit his Centre nonetheless and, at Alex's suggestion, a compromise was agreed whereby the Jordanian Centre was provisionally elected, its election to be confirmed at the next meeting provided that at least three more writers had by then been persuaded to sign the Charter.

This duly happened in New York the following January, but no more was heard of Mr. Abdel Fattah Toukan or his Centre until, oddly, after the fatwa had been pronounced against Salman Rushdie. I was then astonished to receive at King Street a request from Mr. Toukan that a copy of *The Satanic Verses* be sent to him since it was unobtainable in Jordan. I hesitated to comply, torn between fear that he might be getting himself into trouble with the Jordanian authorities and suspicion that he intended to make money out of selling the book privately. In the end I decided that he might just be doing his bit to encourage freedom of expression, so I sent the book in a plain cover. No acknowledgment was ever received.

A more significant event in the Assembly at San Marino was the unopposed choice of Francis as International President Designate to succeed Per at the New York Congress the following January. It should not have been the turn of another Englishman to be President since V. S. Pritchett had only retired from that post in 1976, but Francis had played such a conspicuous and useful part for so long as the voice of reason in International PEN meetings and the champion redrafter of badly phrased resolutions that he was chosen by popular acclaim. English PEN very properly took no part in proposing his candidature, which was put forward by Bob den Doolaard and the Croatian PEN.

A nostalgic note, for me, was struck by the tributes on the death of Carlos de Radzitzky, the flamboyant Belgian baron who had been an outstanding figure at International PEN meetings since well before my time. Amongst other, more affectionate, tributes, Per, not seeking to gloss over his profound disagreement with Carlos's generally Right Wing and reactionary political views, said that Carlos's frequent interventions in the Assembly had "often been astounding and sometimes appropriate".

Another death of a PEN stalwart occurred as a direct result of the Conference. San Marino, as an independent republic within Italy, has always been a haven for refugees. One of those, at the end of the eighteenth century was the physician, necromancer and confidence trickster, Count Cagliostro. He died in San Leo, a fortress town a few miles from the town of San Marino, but within the Republic, and it was there we were taken on a day's excursion at the end of the Conference. Since PEN members, when not discussing literary matters, are dedicated shoppers, many of them bought, as a souvenir of San Leo, bottles of a liqueur with a picture of Cagliostro on the label. Unfortunately it was not the elixir of perpetual youth which the Count claimed to have discovered. Andri Peer, a big, bluff man who wrote in the minority Romansch language and was President of the tiny Swiss Italian Romansch PEN Centre, bought a bottle, and carried it back to his native mountains. On his first evening home he drank some of the liqueur and, whether or not as a direct consequence, dropped dead of a heart attack.

The same liqueur also had a powerful, though fortunately not fatal, effect on Josephine when she and Francis and I drank some on the first evening of the motoring holiday we took in Umbria and Tuscany immediately after the Conference. I think I sank into a stunned sleep, but she was kept awake all night by the thundering of her heart. Francis, perhaps afraid of the liqueur's possible aphrodisiac effect on his female companions, prudently locked his bedroom door!

We did not hear the tragic news about Andri Peer until we got home, but nevertheless decided that it would be wiser to leave Cagliostro's potion for the chambermaid at our first hotel and then set out happily for Urbino in the car which we had hired in Rimini. We were encouraged by the fact that Mimy had given us an introduction to a professor at the University of Urbino, who, she said, would be expecting us and would provide us with accommodation in one of the student residences.

When we arrived there the professor in question was away and we were met by a worried reception committee of academics who clearly knew nothing about us but were too polite to say so. After hurried consultation they gave us student rooms in little wooden houses outside the campus. These were functional, but quite adequate and had a fine view from the back out over the old city. The room Josephine and I shared had a nameplate on the door which said "Mr. Balloo" and we had visions of an earnest, bespectacled African graduate student arriving back in the middle of the night to reclaim his accommodation. No such excitement occurred, and we slept undisturbed.

The only mishap I recall from our very enjoyable holiday was when I succumbed to a nettle rash. We were spending some nights at a delightful pensione up in the hills somewhere in Tuscany, where our hosts, suitably impressed by Francis's scholarly appearance, always referred to him as "il professore". Since I am tiresomely prone to allergies, it may have been something growing in the flowering meadows surrounding the pensione which caused my face to itch and swell, or it may have been something I ate at lunch at the very good restaurant recommended in Francis's guide book. Certainly my rash came on while we were having lunch and disabled me from driving our party home to the pensione. Since Francis does not drive, Josephine had to take over from me, which was brave of her since her own car at that time was an ancient, much-loved Morris Minor so she was unused to the controls of a more modern car. She was also unused to driving on the right. However, as usual, she valiantly took up the challenge and drove us back, with Francis beside her in the passenger seat and me huddled miserably in the back with a face like a Hallowe'en pumpkin. Even in my semi-conscious state I was aware of occasional altercations in front of me:

Francis, nervously: "Josephine, you're driving too close to the edge".
Josephine, indignantly: "Would you rather I drove in the middle of the road?"

Francis is an excellent navigator but, being a non-driver, does not always see matters from the driver's point of view, so that when the car is approaching a multiple junction, with several cars behind and other approaching from every direction, and the driver is urgently asking for instructions, he is apt to say "Wait a moment" whilst he earnestly studies the map. We found the Italian drivers surprisingly patient with us.

7

KEVIN FITZGERALD   St. Moritz Hotel, New York
Crossways, Chinnor, Oxon   January 1986

Dear Kevin,
This hotel has a delightful view over Central Park and is falling to
bits – literally! A piece of plaster fell from the ceiling onto Peter's
head last night, lightly grazing his forehead. When he mischievously
rang the desk and said that the ceiling had fallen on him and he was
bleeding the Manager – obviously accustomed to litigious American
guests – came speeding up accompanied by the hotel lawyer as well
as the doctor. It took him some time to realise that Peter was not
intending to sue. Much love, Elizabeth

Another mark of the St. Moritz's decline was the extreme slowness
of the lifts. This had the advantage that delegates could, whilst waiting
for the lift to arrive, hold ad hoc committee meetings and settle possible disputes before they came up in the Assembly. Rather more tiresome was the frequent wearing away of the metallic strips on the key
cards so that I spent a lot of time unsuccessfully trying to gain access
to my room and then having to go down to reception to get a new
card. This was also a social activity since so many other people were
having the same problem.

Since I arrived a day or two before the start of the Congress I
thought it would be a good idea to telephone Josephine and advise
her to bring a screwdriver because that seemed to be the only way of
adjusting the radiators in the bedrooms. I should have realised that
she never travelled without one. More usefully, I was also able to
warn her that it was much milder in Manhattan than I had imagined
it would be. I had come prepared for snow and ice, with a new, red,
military-style overcoat, a fur hat and fur boots, and found myself
overdressed.

Since the reason for my early arrival at Congresses was to liaise with
the host Centre, I paid a visit to American PEN's new headquarters on
Broadway. The offices were light and bright and spacious, seeming,
to my envious eye, to be about ten times the size of our premises at

King Street. There were certainly many more people working there, each with their own little empire, although under the tight control of Karen Kennerly, their Executive Director, who had been the *éminence grise* of American PEN delegations at International PEN Congresses for some time, but whom I had never before seen on her home ground. Considering that my presence was really supererogatory to what was obviously a very finely-tuned operation, she made me feel welcome and invited me to join her and her mother at a lunch of salad and yoghourt which her mother brought in to the office. Having long admired, from a distance, Karen's beautiful, and obviously expensive, clothes and her fashion plate figure, I was not surprised to discover that her mother was a dress designer.

Alex, though he is a complete cosmopolitan, who is equally at home with races as diverse as the Greeks, the Russians, the Chinese and the Koreans and, although he and Nadia lived for some years in New York, was never on good terms with American PEN. On one thing, however, he and Karen were united and that was a love of dancing, at which they both excelled. At any Congress which included a Ball they would at some stage come together, all their differences forgotten, performing miracles of grace and agility.

The New York Congress, however, did not include a Ball, although there were some splendid parties. One, for a privileged few, took place in the apartment of one of American PEN's wealthiest supporters. In those days there were many such, who were willing to pay vast sums (by our standards) to brush shoulders at fund-raising dinners with famous writers, and this was the chief source of the PEN Centre's income. Our host on this occasion was Sol Steinberg and I believe he had stipulated that certain well-known American writers must be included in the guest list, so that, as well as being dazzled by Gayfrid Steinberg's shoulder-length diamond earrings, and the corresponding opulence of the apartment, one could also stumble upon the likes of Kurt Vonnegut admiring the Rubens and Francis Bacons on the walls. In my innocence, I thought these were all originals, but Peter assured me that the Rubens at any rate were fakes.

A more enjoyable party, this time for everyone, was held in that spectacular recreation of ancient Egypt in the Metropolitan Museum of Art, the Temple of Dendur. This sticks in my memory both because of the stunning effect of the temple set in an artificial lake and because Josephine and I had to guide Harold Harris carefully round the lake on our way out. Harold, then Managing Director of Hutchinson's and very active on the English PEN Committee, had enjoyed himself rather too much at the party, but was one of those rare people who are even more charming when drunk. He was a handsome man, tall and prematurely silver-haired, and looked even more impressive topped with the fur hat which he, like me, had thought suitable for New York in January. "Darlings!", he exclaimed, throwing his arms affectionately round us as we steered him past the water. He was staying either with friends or at a Club, but we saw him safely home in a cab before ourselves returning to the St. Moritz. Next day he had no recollection at all of how he had got home from the party, and we thought it more tactful not to enlighten him.

Norman Mailer was the President of American PEN at the time of the Congress and lent some additional colour to it by appearing with a black eye, said to have been acquired in a bout with a prize fighter. He was very unpopular with the feminist faction in American PEN, who held him responsible for the dearth of women amongst the very distinguished list of guests of honour and therefore frequently interrupted the proceedings by shouting at him. Luckily he is not a man to be fazed by such behaviour. He probably found it stimulating. There were even longer and louder protests outside New York Public Library before the Opening Ceremony. This was because the choice of Secretary of State George Schultz to be the keynote speaker was considered by the protesters to be a political statement, although it seemed to most of us quite appropriate to the theme of the Congress, which was "The Writer's Imagination and the Imagination of the State".

Perhaps, in view of all this shouting, it was lucky that the Assembly of Delegates was, for once, very much a side-show to the literary sessions which had all the star speakers. The Assembly was held in a small conference hall away from the general turmoil, and it was in this more sane and sober atmosphere that Francis's election as International President was confirmed.

Peter tells me that one of the French delegates to the previous New York Congress (held in 1966) commented wryly to the next meeting that the Congress had been an American event to which a few Europeans had been invited. Certainly in 1986 International PEN had very much to take a back seat to American PEN. Although the President of the host Centre at a Congress is normally expected to treat the International President as an honoured guest, Francis remarked that Norman Mailer barely acknowledged him.

*

Immediately after the Congress Josephine, Tony Babington, Peter and I flew to Los Angeles, where Peter hired a car and drove us up the spectactular coast road to San Francisco, where he had arranged to meet Barbara.

We spent our first night in the luxury of the Athenaeum on the beautiful campus of CalTech by kind arrangement with the PEN Centre in Los Angeles (a more successful arrangement than Mimy's with the University of Urbino). From there we drove on to the attractive town of Santa Barbara, where the custodian of the handsome court house, was very impressed to be visited by an English judge and, thanks to the status conferred on us by Tony, gave us a guided tour.

The next night we spent at a motel at a place with the picturesque name of Moonstone Beach. Peter told us that if we fixed our eyes on the setting sun at the exact moment it sank into the Pacific we should see that rare phenomenon, the green flash. Excited by this prospect, we obediently sat in a row on a seat outside the motel, gazing towards the horizon. I regret to say that, although the sun sank into a cloudless sky, there was no green flash. To our sceptical comments, Peter maintained that he had himself seen the green flash over the Indian Ocean and it was thought to be due either to an optical illusion or to the effect of the momentary combination of the yellow of the sun with the blue of the sea.

This was one disappointment. Another, less celestial, was the absence of hash browns for breakfast. It was not until we got to The Beresford Hotel in San Francisco that we managed to get a full American breakfast. At the motels on our route all we got for breakfast was "coffee and a Danish", the coffee drunk standing up out of a plastic beaker as we paid our bills.

Hearst Castle, that extraordinary creation of the newspaper tycoon William Randolph Hearst, immortalised by Orson Wells in "Citizen Kane", did not disappoint. We left our car at the gates and took the bus for the five-mile drive through the grounds, which were stocked, like a game park, with herds of zebra and giraffe. The castle, which looked like a Walt Disney creation, contained an odd mixture of fake Greek and Roman statues, icons, tapestry and furniture, as well as William Randolph Hearst's private cinema and various mementoes of his megalomaniac existence.

Our immediate goal after that was Pacific Grove, where Peter's younger brother, Winston, lives with his English wife, Joan, and their Down's Syndrome son Christopher. We stayed in a motel down on the shore because there was not room for us all in the Elstobs' house, but Winston, a delightfully starry-eyed enthusiast for many causes, did the honours of Pacific Grove, proudly showing us round the Steinbeck Museum which he and a friend had started in the house where the writer had lived for a time, as well as a more eccentric collection of objects connected with the legend of Camelot and King Arthur,

Winston being a believer in the once and future king. He also took us out to Point Sur, a sighting point for blue whales on their migration to and from Mexico. At that season they were on their way south and this time, unlike our sunset vigil for the green flash, we were lucky; we not only saw a school of whales, but also saw some of them breaching, their bodies showing clear above the sea like gigantic salmon leaping. Just how lucky we were we realised when a woman who was on the Point with us said that she had been coming for years to watch the whales' migration, but had never before seen them breaching.

From Pacific Grove Peter drove us to San Francisco and, after having shown us the sights, put us on a plane and at the same time met Barbara's flight out from England. As we returned home they drove back to Pacific Grove, then travelled on to Hawaii, where another of the Elstob clan (one of Peter's half-sisters) lived, before they too flew home. Peter had been feeling increasingly unwell the whole time with undiagnosed diabetes, which brought on the major heart attack he suffered in June, just as the rest of us were foregathering in Hamburg for the next PEN Congress.

8

Dear Kevin,
I think I've been given the honeymoon suite in this beautiful hotel.
The bed is large enough to accommodate a whole delegation (I haven't
yet decided which one!) and there's a circular bath tub. Harold Harris,
who is one of the English delegates, is fascinated to see the modern
city since he was last here with the army of occupation in 1945 when
it had been destroyed by the Allied bombing. Other male delegates
are more interested in the Reeperbahn – for sightseeing only, I think!
Much love, Elizabeth

Alex and I arrived in Hamburg a day or two early, as usual, to
view the arrangements and try to soothe the nerves of the Congress
organisers. In this case the principal organisers were Gerd E. Hoff-
mann and Angelika Mechtel. They were in the usual state of high
tension which Congress organisers suffer just before the big event,
Gerd more so than Angelika. Alex employed all his diplomatic
skills in talking to Gerd, but said to me afterwards that it was like
"stroking a sleeping tiger". Fortunately Ursula Setzer had just started
her long stint as Administrative Secretary of West German PEN and
her efficiency and charm caused Alex to dub her the angel of the
Congress.

It was when we were all assembling for the delegates' lunch at the
Hotel Atlantic before the Assembly opened there that a message
reached me at the hotel from Diana, at International Headquarters,
that Peter had had a major heart attack and his chances of survival
were slim. I walked across the gardens to the Congress Centre in a
state of shock and blurted out the news to the first person I saw,
which luckily was Margareta Ekström. She was very sympathetic and,
probably sensing that I was on the verge of tears, steered me towards
Per as an old friend and a calming influence. He coped admirably,
putting me between himself and the wall at lunch at a table with Alex
and Nadia and Lev Kopelev, the heavily bearded Russian guest of

honour, keeping up a constant flow of conversation on general topics which did not require an answer from me.

Embarrassingly, it was during the afternoon session of the Assembly, when, as minute-taker, I was seated in my usual place on the platform, in full view of all the delegates, that tears started to stream down my face and I could not restrain them. Francis, in the Chair, had commenced the session by announcing Peter's illness and expressing the Assembly's good wishes for his recovery, so the delegates must have been well aware of the cause of my distress. I was never more conscious of the comfort of being amongst friends and was cheered by an encouraging wink from Georges Sion, who, as President of the Francophone Belgian Centre, had his alphabetical place in the front row. With his dapper figure and neat little moustache I have always felt he might easily have been the model for Hercules Poirot.

I was also consoled by Martin, who was attending the Congress as an official delegate of American PEN, together with Norman Mailer's successor as President, Hortense Calisher. He took me out to a restaurant with a balcony overlooking a stretch of water, where we ate an unexpectedly delicious dish of eels.

I should have known that it would take more than a heart attack, however severe, to kill off Peter, who had had so many brushes with death, whether in Barcelona Prison in the Spanish Civil War or fighting his way across Europe in the Tank Corps in the Second World War or at the hotel in Nairobi when it was blown up in January 1981. He had a quintuple bypass, was put on insulin for his diabetes, and made a good recovery.

Some important decisions were taken in the Hamburg Assembly. Alex was re-elected for another four years as International Secretary, and Michael Scammell, who had announced in New York that he would be retiring in Hamburg after ten years as Chairman of the Writers in Prison Committee, agreed to stay on till the following year's Congress, in Lugano, to give more time for a successor to be found. Bob den Doolaard, on the other hand, did retire from being Chairman of the Foundation PEN Emergency Fund. Since the creation of the Foundation in Holland in 1971 he had enlivened the meetings of the Assembly with his reports on the Foundation's covert operations, smuggling financial and other assistance to the families of imprisoned writers, and his retirement was an emotional moment. After thanking all those who had helped the Foundation in its early days, particularly Heinrich Böll, Bob, who had always had a discriminating eye for pretty women, turned to Louise Gareau Desbois, as one of the Foundation's most constant supporters and, in a typically dramatic gesture, descended from the rostrum to embrace her.

When I later asked the Dutch poet and novelist Henk Bernlef what it had been like to succeed Bob as Chairman of the Foundation, he told me, with a wry smile, that on his first mission, which had been to Poland, Bob had enjoined upon him the absolute necessity for preserving the incognito of his local contacts. He must be very careful how he approached them. On this occasion he was to meet his contact at some designated spot (I think it was a newspaper kiosk) on Warsaw railway station and was to carry a tube of embrocation. Bearing this distinguishing mark and standing where he had been told to, he waited for a long time but no-one turned up. Deciding that this was a waste of time, he went to his hotel, where, as he had expected, someone made contact with him to collect the money he was carrying. Ironically, the man who had been supposed to meet him at the railway station had apparently been prevented from doing so by illness. He had bronchitis so would no doubt have benefited from the embrocation to rub on his chest.

It is interesting now to look back on the discussion held in the Hamburg Assembly as to whether or not Nelson Mandela's name should be added to the Writers in Prison Committee's list of prisoners for whom they were working. The proposal was made by Walter Kaufmann on behalf of the GDR Centre and was strongly supported for emotional reasons by many delegates. Others pointed out that, although Mandela was indeed the author of a book, he was in prison for espousing a policy of violence, which put him beyond the scope of PEN's mandate. Michael Scammell also pointed out that if this proposal were accepted a precedent would have been established which would inevitably extend the Writers in Prison Committee's list to an unmanageable length, since almost all political prisoners had written a book at some stage of their career. Josephine sensibly suggested that Mandela's name be added to the list as an investigation case, and this recommendation was accepted.

Michael subsequently presented to the Lugano meeting the conclusion he had come to. This was that since Mandela had advocated violence, he could not qualify for inclusion on the Writers in Prison Committee list. Josephine once again suggested an acceptable compromise, a resolution, put forward on the grounds of PEN's commitment to the support of freedom and opposition to all racism and apartheid, which urged the South African Government to release Mandela.

A more contentious issue at Hamburg, and one that was the beginning of a damaging split in PEN was whether or not another Congress should be held in Seoul in 1988. Korean PEN's invitation had been gladly accepted at the Tokyo Congress two years previously, but since then writers and journalists had been imprisoned in South Korea and there had been reports that some of them had been tortured and some publications suppressed. The move for the cancellation, or at least postponement, of the Congress was spearheaded by American PEN and strongly supported by the Scandinavian Centres. Thomas von Vegesack argued that if PEN held a Congress in a country where there were writers in prison it would cease to be regarded as a serious writers' organisation and become merely a tourist agency.

The basic division of opinion was between those who agreed with Thomas that PEN should never hold a Congress in a country where there were writers in prison and those who felt that the publicity engendered by a PEN Congress was more likely to make the government in the country concerned more sensitive to international public opinion and hence more inclined to release the imprisoned writers. Antonio Olinto pointed out that the latter was exactly what had happened at the 1979 Rio Congress. The military regime then in power in Brazil had released six political prisoners, four of whom were writers, and he was sure that this had been due to interviews given to the press by Michael Scammell.

Alex, controlling his anger at Thomas's gibe about the danger of PEN degenerating into a tourist agency, and his partisanship for Korean PEN, proposed a constructive compromise. Korean PEN, in whom he urged the Assembly to place their confidence, should be requested to produce by the end of the year a full report on all the cases of imprisonment of writers and suppression of publications which had been raised at this meeting. A decision could then be taken as to whether or not the Congress should be proceeded with.

The whole discussion was bedevilled by the consideration that it takes a minimum of two years to prepare a Congress and, unless that Congress is to take place in one of the Western democracies, there can be no guarantee that the regime will not change for the worse within those two years. Should PEN therefore only ever hold meetings in the Western democracies? This would greatly limit its scope and undermine its claim to be an international organisation. It is a question which has never been satisfactorily resolved.

The Hamburg Congress finished on a happier note, with a trip down the Elbe in a smart vessel flying the Congress flag. Somewhere in the course of the trip we moored and an impromptu dance took place on the quayside. I must have been relieved of my anxiety about Peter because I remember dancing (an activity I have to be very light-hearted or rather drunk to indulge in) with Martin and with Predrag Matvejevic, the Croatian writer, newly elected an International Vice-President.

9

KEVIN FITZGERALD   *Lugano*
Crossways, Chinnor, Oxon   *May 1987*

Dear Kevin,
I've helped to destroy the International President's reputation! Francis
came on here from a conference in Bled and somehow got separated
from his luggage en route. So that he could be decent for breakfast
in his room I lent him a white towelling bathrobe from my room, a
transaction which the chambermaids may have misinterpreted, as they
must also have noted the appearance in his room a few nights later
of a high-heeled woman's shoe in a very small size. What happened
to the other shoe? Who was the woman? It's a mystery! Much love,
Elizabeth

Lugano is a lovely place to be at any time of the year, but particularly
in May. Before the Congress started Alex took me and the two Poles,
Juliusz Zulawski and Artur Miedzyrzecki (who were there as observers
only since their Centre was still dormant) on a tour of the marvellous
art collection of Baron Thyssen-Bornemiza. Since then the collection
has gone to the Prado in spite of Prince Charles' efforts to bring it to
England, but in 1987 it was still housed in the Villa Favorita, with
its beautiful gardens overlooking the lake and at that season of the
year ablaze with rhododendrons and azaleas. This must have been
a very soothing escape for the Poles from their troubles with their
government, and for me it was certainly very educative as well as
enjoyable. Alex is a passionate art lover and has the knack, in each
room of any gallery, of immediately singling out the most significant
painting and explaining why it is so. He once took me to the National
Gallery, which after all is only just round the corner from King Street,
for what was supposed to be the first of a series of visits but, either
because he found me a dull pupil, or because we were always too
busy in the office, we never completed the course.

    Like Per before him, Francis was an excellent Chairman of the
Assembly, firm but fair. He was also polite and conscientious in
returning thanks to the hosts of receptions given in PEN's honour.

There was one day, however, when we had been ferried across the lake to be entertained by the Mayor of the neighbouring town of Campione, when Francis's good manners were tried to the limit. The Mayor had laid on a delicious buffet lunch for the delegates, who, behaving, as usual, as if they had not been fed for weeks, started stripping the board while Francis was still in the middle of his speech of thanks. Although the assault on the food was going on behind his back, he could not but be aware of the clink of plates and glasses, and it was a mark of his self-control that his eloquence barely faltered.

The hosts of the Lugano Congress were the Swiss Italian Romansch PEN Centre, now under the presidency of the television writer and producer, Grytzko Mascioni. It was a heroic effort for such a small Centre, with very little money, to host a Congress. Their agreeing to undertake it was another proof of the success of Alex's arts of persuasion. Their success in doing so, however, was due to the charming personality and dynamic efficiency of Grytzko's secretary, Lucia Ambrogini. Lucia had been detached from her job at the television company to organise the Congress and had enlisted the help of a band of equally delightful and attractive female friends, who threw themselves with gusto and enjoyment into running an exemplary Congress and were great fun to work with. Alex was charmed and fascinated by them. I think it gave him a more favourable view of lesbianism.

The most significant event at Lugano was the election of Thomas von Vegesack to succeed Michael Scammell as Chairman of the Writers in Prison Committee. It was a great change in style. Michael was a consummate performer in the Assembly, excellent at marshalling his facts and dealing with objections, but always cool and collected. Thomas, on the other hand is a very passionate fighter against injustice, and, when he represented Swedish PEN, was always wanting to make one more point in the Assembly in spite of the ruling that delegates could only speak once on any particular topic and then make one reply. From my seat on the platform I would often see Thomas leaping around at the back of the meeting and waving his arms to catch the Chairman's attention. In fact Alex once said to Per, when he was International President: "Can't you control your Baltic baron?", referring to Thomas's aristocratic origins in the Baltic States. Electing him to office was rather like appointing a poacher to protect the lord of the manor's game coverts, but it worked very well and made meetings of the Assembly much calmer.

Another inescapable difference between the two men was that Michael had the advantage of being a native English speaker, whereas Thomas, who is fluent in German and French, is brave, but uncertain, in his use of English. His favourite English expletive, which those of us who worked with him in the office came to wait for appreciatively, is "Oh my Godness!". He was also teased about his pronunciation of the word "gaol". Ronald Harwood, a later International President, said he had often wondered in listening to Thomas's reports on the work of the Writers in Prison Committee what all those Turkish and Vietnamese writers were doing in Yale! It was one of the many nice things about Thomas that he took this teasing in good part.

It had been a stormy meeting of the Writers in Prison Committee in Lugano which led up to Thomas's election, with strong resentment on the part of some Centres (chiefly the Americans and Scandinavians) to what they thought was authoritarian interference by International Headquarters in the choice of the Committee's Chairman. This had even led to the proposal to remove from the new guidelines of the Committee the proviso that the International President and Secretary should be consulted in the choice of a Chairman. By the time the Assembly met tempers had cooled and Susan Sontag (a guest of honour from American PEN) made a generous apology to those who had been offended and proposed the reinstatement of that proviso in the guidelines. This olive branch was gracefully accepted by Francis.

Alex also struck a conciliatory note in his report to the Assembly, conjuring up an "Alice in Wonderland" vision of PEN when he said that he sometimes felt that we were all merely puppets in the dream of the English lady who had founded the organisation in the Twenties. Whatever else divided us, we were deeply together in facing up to the formidable enemy of reality, he said, and were buttressed by goodwill.

This goodwill was tested when the issue of the Korean Congress was once more raised. René Tavernier, as enthusiastic an advocate for Korea as Alex, made a passionate appeal for the Congress to be allowed to go ahead as International PEN's best chance to bring more freedom of speech to South Korea and to help the writers there. He besought the Assembly not to kick Korean PEN in the teeth, not to turn the Land of the Morning Calm into the Land of the Sad Twilight.

The effect of René's eloquence was somewhat diluted by the Secretary of Korean PEN, Hyun Bok Lee, who rose to describe the preparations in hand for the Congress without making any reference to the abuses of human rights alleged by those Centres which opposed the Congress. Professor Lee's English was fluent and grammatical, but unfortunately spoken in an Oxbridge drawl (presumably acquired in the language laboratory in which he had learnt it) which had the effect of alienating his listeners. His fellow-delegate, Sang-Deuk Moon, a man of great charm who had acquired his English as a student at Edinburgh University, was a far better advocate for the Korean PEN cause. He was so good in fact that Theophilos Frangopoulos (back in our midst once more, having recovered from his San Marino tantrum) said that, having been against the Korean Congress, listening to Sang-Deuk Moon had changed his mind. He had recognised, he said, a cry from the heart, a moving and unspoken appeal to the delegates to come to Korea and say what Korean writers could not say for themselves.

At the end of a long discussion in which no-one (except Mr. Frangopoulos) was persuaded to change their minds, a vote was taken on a proposal by American PEN that the Congress be postponed "until such time as the climate in South Korea seemed more propitious for the enterprise". It was defeated by a majority of 15, with 3 abstentions.

With this time-bomb left ticking, the Assembly passed to the consideration of other less controversial future meetings. The next Congress was to be in San Juan, Puerto Rico, in December, the one after that in Maastricht in April 1989 (before that town in southern Holland had become better known for a different sort of conference). Joost de Wit, in putting the latter invitation on behalf of the Netherlands PEN, among other inducements to delegates to Maastricht, said that the bars there stayed open all night. Francis, in thanking Joost, swiftly picked him up on this point, asking him to arrange for the bars to be shut for at least some of the night. It was difficult enough to get the Assembly together at 9 o'clock in the morning without that additional hazard, Francis commented.

The literary theme at Lugano was, appropriately considering the situation, "Border Literatures". I regret to say that my only recollection of the discussions is that René Tavernier, who was on one of the panels, made far too long a speech then, without waiting to listen to his fellow-panelists, gathered up his possessions in a string bag and stumped off the stage. Michael Holroyd, then President of English PEN, whose manners are always impeccable, was so shocked by this rudeness that he could never bring himself to appreciate the more engaging side of René's personality. Even now, he says, he remembers René's "endless speech on Chateaubriand – it took a minute every time he pronounced the name".

Tim Heald was also in Lugano, having been given, as he himself described it, the "grand, rather Ruritanian, not to say vainglorious" title of International Coordinator, with the job of fund-raising for the Writers in Prison Committee. It was he who thought up – needless to say, not as part of his official duties – the idea of a revolving stage for future literary sessions, so that over-verbose delegates could be smoothly transported, still talking, into another room, where they could complete their speech to their own satisfaction whilst the next speaker took the floor in the main conference hall. Sadly, it has never proved possible to implement this brilliant scheme.

*

After a rather jolly post-Congress excursion up into the Swiss Alps with a motley selection of other delegates, Josephine, Tony, Francis and I were dropped off the excursion bus and made our way to Bellagio, beautifully situated on Lake Como at the point where it divides into two arms. From our pleasant pensione there we made various excursions by lake steamer, including one to the next town, where there was a dentist. This was because poor Josephine had an abscess on a tooth which even she – brought up to be stoical about pain – could scarcely bear. Francis acted as interpreter for her, but unfortunately the dentist did not give her a strong enough antibiotic, and she continued in agony and unable to sleep at nights (as I, who shared a room with her, was well aware) throughout our return journey to Milan, where we caught out plane home. So one of our most enjoyable Congresses ended, for her, in Casualty at Charing Cross Hospital, where I took her immediately we got back to Fulham, and where the doctors greeted her with dismay and very strong antibiotics, saying that, had she not come to them when she did the infection from the abscess would have poisoned her whole system.

10

KEVIN FITZGERALD
Crossways, Chinnor, Oxon

San Juan
December, 1987

Dear Kevin,
Alex is very clever at persuading PEN Centres in delightful places that
they want to host Congresses. The Puerto Rican Centre has been
inactive for years, but has been reinvigorated by a wiry-haired little
professor called Luis Nieves Falcon, who is a ball of energy and has
invited us here to this Caribbean island to discuss the role of the hero
(or heroine) in the novel of the Americas – part of a wider Unesco
project, as you might have guessed – to admire the Spanish colonial
architecture of old San Juan, and to enjoy bountiful Puerto Rican
hospitality. Much love, Elizabeth.

The pattern of PEN's international meetings had hitherto been one
Congress a year (numbered in sequence from the very beginning)
with sometimes an additional smaller meeting, called an International
Conference. There had been wartime years when there were no Congresses and sometimes since then one had been cancelled, usually
because the host Centre found they could not afford it, and so the
pattern had been broken, but there had never been two Congresses
in one year except for 1986, when the New York Congress had slipped
over from 1985 into the following January to suit American PEN's
financial arrangements. The San Juan meeting had originally been
scheduled as a Conference, but Luis Nieves Falcon asked that it
be elevated to the status of the 51st Congress because that sounded
more important and made fund-raising easier. When the Assembly
agreed to his request they created a precedent. Everyone henceforward
wanted their meeting to be a Congress, so, except for the Cambridge
meeting the following spring, there were no more International Conferences. This seemed to me a pity since I had always enjoyed Conferences more than Congresses as being more intimate and informal
gatherings.

The San Juan Congress, however, retained the virtues of a Conference. Because of the expense of travel from Europe, there were fewer

delegates than usual at a Congress and so the parties were smaller and it was easier to get to know people. Indeed there was certainly an intimate and informal moment on the last morning, when, as they sat side by side in the jacuzzi by the hotel pool, Walter Kaufmann expatiated to Josephine on the charms of a beautiful Puerto Rican girl he had met at a party the previous night. He wanted to give up everything for love. Sadly, reality must have intervened because when he came to the following year's Conference in Cambridge it was still as a delegate of the East German Centre.

The argument about the Korean Congress was inevitably renewed, but, as was appropriate at a Latin American meeting, the chief drama in the Assembly concerned Chile. The President and sole delegate of Chilean PEN, Eliana Cerda de Jarnholt, protested indignantly against a resolution demanding that the Chilean dictatorship cease to harass and threaten journalists for exercising their right to freedom of speech. She said that Chile was not a dictatorship. By the 1973 coup General Pinochet had saved his country from a terrible fate. Chile was a small country struggling to survive in spite of the menace of Marxism. Journalists who ridiculed the President and the armed forces were breaking the law and that was why they had been brought before the courts, but they had then been released with a caution.

There followed two different versions of a recent visit which Bernice Rubens had paid to Chile. Josephine said that Bernice had reported to a recent meeting of the English PEN Committee that she had been horrified to discover the terrible events which were taking place behind a façade of normality. Eliana rejoined that she had entertained Bernice several times in her house and Bernice had told her that she had been very surprised by what she had seen on her visit and by the amount of freedom of expression in Chile. It evidently had not occurred to Eliana that this was an ambiguous statement.

Inevitably the resolution was adopted with only Eliana voting against it. The reaction of the other delegates to her defence of Pinochet reminded me of the days when Henryk Keisch used often to be the only spokesman for the communist regimes and similarly spoke into a shocked silence. This time the silence did not last. Amongst the In-Session Resolutions put forward the next day was one from the Catalans, the Swedes and the Flemish which called upon Chilean PEN to reaffirm its commitment to the Charter and to demonstrate that commitment by acting in defence of the writers in Chile who were persecuted and imprisoned for exercising their right to freedom of expression. The resolution finished with a threat of dire consequences if the Chilean PEN did not produce a full report on all these cases by the end of the following month.

There followed a heated argument in which some delegates said that they feared for the future of PEN if it allowed a Centre which so flagrantly identified with its government to continue to exist, and others deplored the inclusion of a threat in what was in fact a family quarrel. Jascha Kessler, from the Los Angeles Centre, expressed the reaction of most of the delegates when he said that he had talked to Eliana and she seemed to be living in a different world. It was finally agreed that the threat be withdrawn and the resolution replaced by a letter to Chilean PEN asking them if what Eliana had said represented the point of view of the Centre and what action they had taken with regard to the persecuted and imprisoned writers. Francis rounded off the discussion in the true spirit of PEN by expressing his admiration for Eliana's courage in defending an unpopular point of view, however misguided that point of view might be. In response Eliana apologised for her intervention the previous day, which she admitted had owed more to sentiment than to reason, and reaffirmed Chilean PEN's commitment to the Charter.

On the last evening we got away from the enclosed space of the conference room and the American tourists clustered round the fruit machines in the lobby of our hotel and drank pina coladas as guests of the Governor of Puerto Rico in the grounds of his mansion, La Fortaleza, part of the fortifications of Old San Juan.

The next day, after Josephine had extracted herself from her interesting conversation with Walter in the jacuzzi, she and Martin and I hired a car and drove off to Luquillo on the north-east corner of the island, the Atlantic shore, where we rented an apartment on the nineteenth floor of a block down on the beach. I sent my mother a post card from there on 7th December (my birthday) in which I said that we were celebrating with coffee and cake and that the climate was warm with a cool breeze. Josephine and I had just driven Martin to the airport for his flight back to New York and were staying on for a few more days of swimming and lazing on the beach. It did not work out quite like that. It must have been just after I posted that card that the wind ceased to be a cool breeze and got up to what felt (at least on the nineteenth floor) like hurricane proportions. Everything in the apartment rattled and banged and we thought the whole block might be blown out to sea. The door to the room Martin had been sleeping in blew shut and resisted all our attempts to open it. Had he not departed for New York, he might be there still.

As usual, I was quite glad to get home to England, where it might be cold and snowy but hurricanes were rare.

11

KEVIN FITZGERALD
Crossways, Chinnor, Oxon

Dakar
January 1988

Dear Kevin,
Here I am back in Senegal five years after my first visit, this time with
representatives of twelve African countries to talk about a new aspect
of oral tradition: "Writing for Radio". Alex and Nadia and I unfortu-
nately arrived at the same time as the travel-stained, but glamorous,
drivers in the Paris to Dakar motor rally, so all the hotels in the city
were crammed and we had to spend our first night in a stinking hole
of an airport hotel. Fortunately we have now been moved to more
acceptable accommodation and await the arrival of Francis. Much
love, Elizabeth

The night the Blokhs and I spent at what passed for an airport hotel
in Dakar had its amusing side. In addition to the rooms being filthy
and ill-lit, the lavatory floors were awash and there was of course no
toilet paper. We had been met on our arrival by the Secretary of
Senegal PEN, Alioune Badara Beye, who had, without apology, con-
signed us to these dismal quarters and said he would come back the
next morning to take us to the conference hotel. When he reappeared
he intercepted Alex on his way back to his and Nadia's room from a
foraging expedition. Nadia and I had meanwhile decided to fill in the
time by having a cup of coffee in the airport café and from our table
we had a clear view of the fascinating sight of Alex and Badara Beye
at another table evidently having a monumental row, totally oblivious
of the roll of pink toilet paper sitting on the table between them.

The whole conference was conducted against a thunderous background of continuing dispute between Alex and Badara Beye, which,
as far as I remember, concerned the financing of the enterprise. It was
Alex who had managed to obtain the finance from Unesco and who
therefore naturally expected to administer it. This was not the view,
however, of Badara Beye who felt that, as Secretary of the host Centre,
he should have the handling of it.

The other members of Senegal PEN were very friendly and I remember with pleasure a poetry reading given at one of their houses, all of them – particularly the ladies – splendidly dressed in their local costume. Apart from Alex, Nadia, Francis and me the other non-African participants were Per and Anita Theorell (who had replaced Margareta as his partner since our last visit to Senegal) and Luis Nieves Falcon – a reward for the success of the Puerto Rican Congress.

My only disagreeable recollection is that, in place of the enterprising salesmen who had pursued Francis, Martin and me in 1983, there was a legless beggar in the main square who dragged himself along at such speed that I became afraid to go out of the hotel on my own. I suppose I should have given him something, but I felt that that would only make him chase me even faster next time I went out.

This time there was no post-conference trip, but, instead of flying straight home I took the TGV from Paris to Avignon (the first time I had travelled on it since we all baptised it at the Lyons Congress in 1991) and joined the Elstobs, who had borrowed Stephen and Natasha Spender's Provençale retreat, Mas St. Jerome, set in its own olive grove. It was still only February, but the sun shone out of a cloudless blue sky. Peter had recovered from his quintuple heart bypass, but was moving gingerly as a result of having broken five ribs in a fall off the edge of the unrailed staircase at Mas St. Jerome onto the night storage heater in the hall. Nevertheless he took Barbara and me on various excursions, including a visit to Arles, where we ate a delicious lunch and admired the bull ring. We also went to lunch with Angus Wilson and Tony Garrett in their penthouse apartment overlooking the market in St. Rémy. Peter had known Angus for many years and the two couples had seen quite a lot of each other since Peter and Barbara had taken up their residence at Mas St. Jerome. Indeed, when Peter had had his fall Tony had been a Good Samaritan and come to the Elstobs' assistance with shopping and cooking since Barbara was still considerably disabled from the stroke she had suffered fourteen years previously. Angus also required a lot of care since he was by this time already very frail and lacking his former sparkle. He was nevertheless a charming host, very gentle and courteous.

*

It can be very cold in Cambridge in April; it certainly was in 1988 when English PEN hosted an International Conference in King's College. We even woke up one morning to find the trees rimed with frost. The people who suffered worst from this unseasonable weather were the French delegation. They had chosen to be quartered in the more romantic seventeenth century student accommodation, with sitting-rooms but only shared bathrooms, rather than in the en suite accommodation in the modern block and it transpired that they did not know how to light the gas fires in their rooms. Obviously gas fires are as alien to the French as airing cupboards. Fortunately Gillian Tindall, who had been given the task of looking after the francophones, sorted this problem out before they froze to death. In general the delegates were very happy to be living in King's College and dining in the beautiful college hall. Since 300 was the maximum that could be accommodated in the college it was, as Josephine had forecast when she issued the invitation, a very family occasion.

When the idea of the Conference was first mooted Josephine had announced to the Organising Committee that she needed someone efficient to cope with the details of the organisation. Gilly Vincent (later to succeed her as Secretary of English PEN), who was a member of the committee, announced that she had a friend, Hazel Pattinson, who she thought would be ideal: elegant, talented, charming, familiar with computers and a good linguist. We all exclaimed that surely such a paragon would cost us more than we could possibly afford, but Gilly rejoined that Hazel had the additional advantage of living with a wealthy man, and therefore being able to take on short-term jobs which interested her without charging more than expenses. We could not believe our luck when Hazel agreed to take on the job and turned out to be everything that Gilly had said she was. She ran the Conference with what appeared to be effortless efficiency. In addition her partner, Peter Francis, kindly came and operated a taxi service from Cambridge Station to King's College. He and I went together to meet the trains from London so that I could greet the delegates and introduce them to him. The only thing that went wrong in all our arrangements was due to the incompetence of a lady volunteer, a friend of Mimy's, who was put in charge of the excursion to Althorp to see the birthplace of the Princess of Wales and allowed the coach driver to take them miles in the wrong direction. The delegates' annoyance was not assuaged by Peter Day pointing out to them that fortuitously the detour had taken them past his birthplace.

There were two moving events in the Assembly. One was the election of a Kurdish Centre (inevitably of Kurds in exile). The application for the Centre was made by the writer for children, Huseyin Erdem, who lives in Cologne. When Huseyin had first come to International Headquarters to talk about this possibility, he had practically no English, but I was quite won over by his wide-eyed, innocent charm. By the time he came to Cambridge he had learnt much more English and, although Alex felt it necessary to warn him that if the Kurdish Centre were to be elected it must be representative of Kurdish writers everywhere and must not be used in a partisan political way, the Assembly too were captivated and voted unanimously for the Centre to come into existence. Huseyin, overcome with gratitude, presented Alex with a red rosebud for his buttonhole.

The second moving event was the speech made by the Russian poet Nizametdin Akhmetov, until the previous year a prisoner in a Soviet psychiatric institution, from which he had been freed only as a result of a massive international campaign on his behalf spearheaded by PEN. (He had been a particular protegé of Kathleen von Simson's.) While he was in prison he had been elected an honorary member of English PEN, among other Centres, and so we had invited him from Germany, where he was now living, to be a guest of honour in Cambridge. At the end of his speech, which he made in Russian and Alex translated, and which was all about forgiving his enemies, Akhmetov said: "Let us look out of the window. There you will find spring, a world reborn. And I want to wish all of you, dear friends, while thanking each of you, a beautiful spring and a love reborn. Let us live for that – freedom, spring, love. And good luck to man everywhere." Francis, when thanking him, said that Akhmetov's speech had undoubtedly been the most moving he, Francis, had ever heard at a PEN Assembly. After that one could almost feel sorry for the Bulgarian delegation, who had obviously come primed to object to the speech as a political gesture, and who ploughed ahead and made the objection as if they had not heard a word Akhmetov had said. Francis replied crisply that their objection would be noted and went on to say that Akhmetov had spoken not as a Soviet prisoner but as representing all prisoners for freedom of expression everywhere.

The final session of the Conference was held in the Lady Mitchell Hall and incorporated Writers' Day, so it was open to the public. It started with a duologue between Iris Murdoch and John Bayley on "Whither the Novel?" and concluded with a speech by Vikram Seth exploring and comparing all the many literary forms in which he has worked.

I had my moment of glory at the beginning of the afternoon when, along with the prizes always awarded on this occasion, I was presented by Antonia Fraser (then President of English PEN) with two handsome cheques (why two? I can't remember) to mark my twenty years' working for PEN. In my speech of thanks I harked back to the two celebratory dinners which had been held for David on his twentieth anniversary sixteen years before (one for English PEN and one for International PEN, at the latter of which Rosamond Lehmann, majestic in silver lamé, had gracefully handed David his presents from the Centres, rather as if the fairy from the top of the Christmas tree had descended to distribute the presents piled at its foot):

"As often on PEN occasions, I wonder what David Carver would have thought of this. After all, he invented the idea of a twentieth anniversary. Probably, knowing David, he would take it as a tribute to his perspicacity that, when he engaged me as his personal secretary in that far-off summer of 1968, he chose someone with such powers of endurance. Really more of the credit should go to Peter, who shored up PEN in the dark days of 1974 when David died and it was on the point of collapse, and gave me the rather grandiloquent title of Administrative Secretary, and to Alex Blokh, who – greatly daring – took over from Peter as the first foreigner to be International Secretary and has done so much for the entente cordiale by his brave endurance of the cramped conditions in our headquarters at the Africa Centre when he descends upon us once a month from Paris. Also, since I've had the good fortune to go on working for the English Centre as well as International PEN, even though the two are now in different premises, I should mention the stimulus of working with Josephine, which would have prevented me giving it up if I'd ever thought of it.

In fact I never have. Staying in the same job for twenty years may sound stick-in-the-mud and dull, but I assure you it hasn't been. It has always been taxing, sometimes infuriating, sometimes rewarding, sometimes hilarious, but never for a moment dull."

I went on to recount a few of the adventures which I've already chronicled in these memories, and then concluded:

"In between all these travels I came back to the relative peace of the English Centre, whether in the crumbling elegance of Glebe House – where the parties given in the glass-domed vine room to launch the poetry anthologies are still remembered nostalgically by a whole generation of poets – or, latterly, in the congenial shabbiness of Dilke Street.

To those of you here who are not PEN members this may all sound rather frivolous. You probably know PEN as a sort of Amnesty International for writers, and indeed it has fought for imprisoned writers and freedom of speech since long before Amnesty was thought of. However, in order to be able to do this – to be any use as a pressure group – it has to fulfil its other calling as an international literary organisation, a family of writers existing across frontiers and language barriers and political divides. It has been that aspect of PEN which it has been my job to serve over the past twenty years, and which I hope to go on serving for a few more years yet."

I did go on for another nine years, but during that time PEN became in a way a victim of its own success, larger and more divided, so, since these memories are entirely a self-indulgent exercise, I will indulge myself by stopping at this pleasant memory of Cambridge in the spring.

APPENDIX
The PEN Charter

The PEN Charter is based on resolutions passed at its international congresses and may be summarised as follows:

PEN affirms that:

1. Literature, national though it be in origin, knows no frontiers, and should remain common currency between nations in spite of political or international upheavals.

2. In all circumstances, and particularly in time of war, works of art, the patrimony of humanity at large, should be left untouched by national or political passion.

3. Members of PEN should at all times use what influence they have in favour of good understanding and mutual respect between nations; they pledge themselves to do their utmost to dispel race, class and national hatreds, and to champion the ideal of one humanity living in peace in one world.

4. PEN stands for the principle of unhampered transmission of thought within each nation and between all nations, and members pledge themselves to oppose any form of suppression of freedom of expression in the country and community to which they belong, as well as throughout the world wherever this is possible. PEN declares for a free press and opposes arbitrary censorship in time of peace. It believes that the necessary advance of the world towards a more highly organised political and economic order renders a free criticism of governments, administrations and institutions imperative. And since freedom implies voluntary restraint, members pledge themselves to oppose such evils of a free press as mendacious publication, deliberate falsehood and distortion of facts for political and personal ends.